Explanation of Natural Events
and Human Actions

Explanation of Natural Events and Human Actions

ARUNA MAZUMDAR

Introduction by
DEBI PRASAD CHATTOPADHYAYA

CHRONICLE BOOKS
An Imprint of DC Publishers

New Delhi
2005

© Aruna Mazumdar 2005

Chronicle Books is an imprint of DC Publishers

Distributed by
Orient Longman Limited
Bangalore Bhopal Bhubaneshwar Chandigarh
Chennai Ernakulam Guwahati Hyderabad Jaipur
Kolkata Lucknow Mumbai New Delhi Patna

ISBN 81-8028-024-1

Typeset in Bembo
by Eleven Arts, New Delhi
Printed in India by Pauls Press, New Delhi
Published by DC Publishers
D-27 NDSE Part II, New Delhi 110 049

DEDICATED TO MY PARENTS

Acknowledgements

I am grateful to the Editor of the *Journal of Indian Council of Philosophical Research* for permission to reproduce some chapters in this book. Section 1 of Chapter One is a slightly altered version of my earlier "Causal Explanation, Deduction and Prediction" and sections 1, 2, 4, 5 of Chapter III "Action and Explanation" have appeared in this journal.

I am indebted to my teachers, friends and relatives who have encouraged me in my academic endeavour. There are a few who deserve special mention. My gratitude to my teacher, Professor D.P. Chattopadhyaya, is immense. Without his help and inspiration, I would never have thought of writing this book. I am grateful to the Indian Academy of Philosophy, Kolkata, who supported my research with a scholarship for three years. The lectures and the discussions I had with the late Professor Chandroday Bhattacharya of the Indian Academy of Philosophy, the late Professor P.K. Sen of Jadavpur University and Shri Durgadas Bandyopadhyay of Calcutta University have helped me in my research.

I also thank D.C. Publishers for publishing this book.

Finally, my greatest debt is to my family—my husband (Bijan Mazumdar), daughter (Priyanka) and (Saswata) son-in-law.

Contents

Introduction

Actions, generally speaking, are of two main types—natural and human. Within these broad types several sub-types are available and discerned. Human actions, for example, may be voluntary, i.e. due to conscious will, or involuntary. Involuntary actions are often viewed under different heads—instinctive, reflex and habitual. The philosophers who believe in the primacy of consciousness, or are panpsychist in their orientation, maintain that the taxonomy of the psychological phenomena should not be pressed beyond a point. For, they argue, all mental phenomena have a common family resemblance between them. The commonness is sought to be explicated in terms of what is called *intention*. Every mental phenomenon is claimed to be informed of an *objectwardness*. In terms of these important concepts of intentionality or objectwardness a well known distinction has been drawn between "what is mental" and "what is physical". The physical action is believed to be *externally* caused, whereas the mental action is said to be *internally* initiated or willed by some or other conscious human agent.

The distinction between what is externally caused and what is internally initiated deserves refinement. Nothing can be externally caused *absolutely* in the human context. Humans by their strength of will or conviction can more or less resist external pressure. Even under duress some strong-willed persons do not buckle. They are prepared even to die for their conviction—religious or scientific. In history of science and history of religion one finds numerous examples to buttress this point.

It is equally interesting to look at this important issue from another end. For example, persons of feeble nature facing difficulties break down easily. In their case the distinction between "constraint" and "coercion" hardly makes any difference. Even if they are put under some or other constraint, they feel coerced and can hardly stand up to it without yielding. The expressions like "strength of will" and "feeble nature", though open to questioning in various ways, are central to both moral philosophy and juridical science. Even at the level of common sense the concepts underlying these terms are extremely important. Human culpability or responsibility cannot be adequately explained without the clarity of these concepts and their surrogates.

The naturalist or reductionist approach to the distinction between "the physical" and "the mental" centers round the concepts like extension, coercion and their affine cognates. Both in the western (e.g., Cartesian—Lockean—Kantian) tradition and the Indian (e.g. Sāṃkhya and Jaina) tradition these two categories of reality are well recognised. This sort of ontological dualism has been frequently highlighted. At the same time attempts have been made to overcome the uncomfortable consequences of this dualism. One is the *reductionist* approach. The other is known as *interactionism*. The third approach is often referred to as *parallelism*. Still a different approach, *reconciliatory* in character, purports to show that "the physical" and "the mental" are subordinate to, and appear to be kindred aspects of one and the same higher principle, God or Absolute. Each of these views has received different formulations in different philosophical or psychological traditions over the centuries.

Reductionism may be physicalist or mentalist. According to the physical reductionist programme, all human body-based disciplines, including biology and psychology, are reducible, at least in principle to the laws of Physics. The main trouble with this view is that it leads to ignore the qualitative distinction between the physical properties and the mental ones. Causally generated problems of physical bodies are not ordinarily evident in the mental phenomena. Besides, dispositional phenomena of the mind can hardly be translated without remainder into purely physical terms. Another problem of the physical reductionist programme is its inability to account for paranormal or extra-sensory mental phenomena like *alaukika* or *yogaja pratyaksa* and its dismissive attitude to the same.

Interactionism, often associated with the name of Descartes (1596–1650), is apparently attractive. But scrutiny reveals its inadequacy and flaws. If two substances are *quite* unlike in their character and composition, it is difficult to conceive of their interaction. Can we rationally think of that physical energy, which is said to be measurable by the physicist, is transformable into mental energy? Psychological phenomena like anger, enthusiasm and excitement, in spite of their overt or visible expressions cannot be easily shown to be *entirely* physicalist in character. Even more difficult is to translate the mental phenomena like peace, mercy and piety into physicalist idioms. It is common knowledge that many people of really composed character and cool disposition remain calm even in the face of grave provocation, temptation and threat. These points indicate the importance of *will* factor of the mind and to which due recognition is not given by the reductionist of the physicalist school.

Among the most well-known parallelists one must mention Spinoza (1632–1677). Opposed to the Cartesian dualism, Spinoza speaks of parallelism between the *extensional* (physical) aspect of God or Nature and its *thought aspect*. According to him, both the finite mode of *extension*, motion-and-rest, and the infinite eternal mode of *thought*, i.e., intellect, and all its modifications, including human knowledge, are embedded in God. Thought and extension are said to be parallel, not interactive. The human mind is said to be the idea of human body and the latter has taken to be extended expression of the human mind. Spinoza's parallelism, unless believed to be rooted in a substantive God which brings about the correspondence between the physical series of extension and the mental series of thought, his theory appears to be confusing. Moreover, Spinoza's word "idea" is highly misleading because it is not attributable to any particular person yet it is said to have its ontological status. Also it is not clear how we, human beings as knower, can apprehend knowledge which itself is claimed to be a part of the *necessary* causal process of the physical world.

In order to remove these anomalies of the Spinozistic view, Leibniz (1646–1716), one of his successors defended the doctrine of the *pre-established harmony*, according to which the mental phenomena or the mental series, on the one end, and the physical phenomena or the physical series, on the other, are *essentially* same. They are said to be "mirror" of each other. In other words, they are *essentially* isomorphic. Unlike Spinoza, Leibniz affirms that matter is mental, that mind is the material, and that God is in both, rather, one may say, both are in God. To him, the difference between divinity, mentality and physicality is only one of degree. Leibniz's *gradualist* theory of the body-mind relation, grounded in an all-pervasive pre-established harmony and supported by the *law of continuity*, is an extension and revision of both Cartesian dualism and Spinozistic parallelism. In effect, his theory is purported to reconstruct a coherent theory of mind and knowledge drawing upon the said two predecessors but differing from them by affirming that physical causalism as ordinarily understood in natural science needs radical revision bringing it in lines with teleological coherentism.

While Descartes derives this dualistic metaphysics from the *cogito*-based epistemology, Spinoza derives his epistemology from the notion of God or Nature. To the latter, God is Nature and Nature is God. This is a kind of European shamanism in which naturalism and spiritualism are interfused. This anticipates Leibniz. Therefore it is not surprising that Spinoza has been interpreted by some philosophers like Novalis as "God-intoxicated", while others like the Marxist regard him as "materialist". However, of Leibniz this cannot be said. And that explains one of the main differences between Newton's causal mechanics and Leibniz's spiritual monadism.

In the body-mind theories of Descartes and Spinoza the main difficulty which one encounters is their common commitment to a strong deductive approach, leading to a bifurcative account of both *physical event* and *mental action*. Leibniz's twin theories of (a) the pre-established harmony and (b) the continuity-based gradualism are purported to unify the uncomfortable consequences of dualism and parallelism. Leibniz finds no fundamental division between "cause of event" and "reason of action". His account of the Law of the Sufficient Reasons is intended to bridge the supposed gap between "physical causality" and "mental rationality". Even cause has sufficient reason in it, ensuring human freedom in the form of *spontaneity* and purged off the blemishes of deterministic necessarianism.

This unified general theory of event and action developed by Leibniz was challenged by Kant (1724–1804) under the twin influences of Newtonian mechanics and the Humean psychology.

Kant basically under the influence of the Cartesian dualism and substantially indifferent to Leibniz's spiritual monadism, develops his ingenious philosophy of two types of the use of reason, theoretical and practical. In his *Critique of Pure Reason* he offers, in brief, a sustained epistemological justification of the Newtonian mechanics. In his early life he claimed that the whole world, together with all its aspects, including events and actions, can be satisfactorily explained in terms of a single principle of matter-in-motion. Later on, his deeper reflection on the nature of free will convinced him that to account for it satisfactorily his justificationist epistemological theory on Newtonian physics would not be enough. Persuaded of the advisability of a different approach, he developed a different epistemology specifically addressed to the free will and actions of human beings. The resulting *Critique of Practical Reason*, though structurally similar to the *Critique of Pure Reason*, differs from it in a very substantial way. Though he accepts the Newtonian thesis of causal determinism, partially supported by Spinoza's account of naturalism, he refuses to accept the view that natural necessity invades the realm of free will and action. In this respect he was somewhat influenced by Hume's criticism of the Newtonian claim that laws of nature are exceptionlessly necessary in the character. Hume's criticism of Newton is basically methodological, not substantive, in character. Hume, following Newton, maintains that though the laws of nature are in themselves necessary in character, this necessity cannot be methodologically established mainly because of the inherent infirmity of induction based on the psychological laws of association. Therefore Hume bases his moral theory on what is called *moral sense* of man and he supplements it by the practically effective force of tradition, convention and custom, which is admittedly contingent.

Kant, significantly influenced by Hume's methodological critique of Newtonian laws, was urgently in need of providing an alternative foundation for the necessity claim of the moral laws he had in his view. In order to avoid the relativism and the contingent character of the moral laws conceived by Hume, Kant had to think of a surer foundation of moral law which would be different from the Humean moral sense attended by social conditions. Understandably that led Kant to a transcendental foundation of the moral law so that it could be categorical or exceptionless. The underlying idea of Kant was to delink moral law from social trend marked by tradition, convention and custom. By implication he tries to clearly delink moral law from scientific law, separating moral actions from the causal series of events.

In philosophy, as we know, old problems often reappear in new guise. The controversy between naturalism and anti-naturalism in the context of natural event and in human action has been of late engaging the attention of many well-known philosophers of different persuasions. Anglo-American philosophers like Wittgenstein, Quine, Davidson and their followers have paid attention to this area. Also of importance is the approach of the European thinkers like Husserl, Heidegger, Sartre and their followers. While the analytic philosophers like Davidson, largely under the influence of Quine, try to show that explanation of action by reason is a species of causal explanation defended by naturalists. At the same, they want to show that mental events are *not* to be treated exactly like natural events for the explanatory purpose. Davidson speaks of a sort of anomalous monism which comprises both body and mind. It is naturalistic monism with a difference and recognizes some borderline phenomena in order to avoid the look of radical reductionism.

Explaining a mental phenomenon like anguish and explaining a bodily event like blood pressure cannot be rendered rationally intelligible in an identical way. For the latter the expert physician, for example, can tell us, or at least the concerned patient, the attending conditions for which he experiences pain. Also he can cure it by administering suitable medicine or advising rest or both. The reason of one's anguish is more or less peculiar to the concerned person.

What causes anguish in one person may not produce that feeling in another. It depends, apart from other things, much on the moral sensibility and attentiveness of the concerned person. It may be added here that neither cause nor reason is an unambiguous term. To offer rational explanation and to give a causal account of an action or event is not necessarily the same or even similar. When we speak of *cause* in the context of law or litigation, it is quite different from what we mean by cause of anguish. For example, in the psychological context often this word is used in the sense of *source*. For example, when we say that the cause of the flood in the lower Gangetic basin is heavy and continuous rain in the upper reaches of the Himalaya and in the catchment areas immediately below the same, we are using the word cause in the sense of source. But in this context *source* is not characterized by unpreventable or exceptionless causal necessity. If in both upper and lower reaches of the river strong and big dams in good number could be constructed, then in spite of heavy rain or downpour by itself cannot cause flood. In that case the term *cause* loses its supposed necessary forces.

The meanings of such expressions as "motive as cause", "cause as justification" and "first cause" are notably different. If these expressions are embedded into sentences of different types and those sentences and the same are *used* by different persons in different context, the meanings of the said expressions differ even more glaringly. I say all these only to highlight the simple point that the Davidsonian view "that rationalization is a species of causal explanation", in spite of its admirable ingenuity and logical subtlety, can be shown to be vulnerable on several counts.

Similar considerations may be offered in explicating various senses of the word "cause". Cause has been used in ordinary English in such widely different senses as "ground", "basis", "determinant", "rationale", "intelligence", "understanding", "brain" and "head". One can easily see that when all these words and their cognates as parts of full-fledged sentences are written or/and spoken, the asymmetry between *cause* and *reason* becomes clear. And in those cases to press the Davidsonian point that to offer *rational* explanation is nothing but to offer a type of *causal* explanation would be idle and unconvincing.

In view of the above considerations it seems to me that to draw a line of distinction between causal explanation in the *naturalist sense* and rational explanation in the *human logical sense* makes good sense. This line of argument also takes us back to the Aristotelian and Leibnizean accounts of different types of causal and telelogical explanation. To ignore this important distinction and to argue for a pro-reductionist approach would be unenlightening.

Dr Aruna Mazumdar's detailed analysis of cause, causal laws, law-statement and laws of nature are both informed and perceptive. The way she has brought the question of freedom to bear upon the issue of causality is indeed very interesting. Her use of logical techniques for explicating causal proposition and inference deserve close perusal for realization of their fuller implications. One may or may not agree or accept her own thesis on the unity or affinity between causal and non-causal explanation but about the high quality of her comprehension and articulation of the concerned views, one must be thankful to her.

Personally speaking, I find her reference to the Indian views on causal explanation very interesting. This scholarly book has been written in a very lucid and readable style.

I am sure that scholars, researchers and the reading public will be profited by reading this monograph.

Debi Prasad Chattopadhyaya

Kolkata

15 August 2004

CHAPTER I

Cause, Explanation and Prediction

The present chapter is devoted to a discussion of the function and nature of the concept of cause. In order to clarify the issue, I propose to discuss certain points. First, I concentrate upon those particular aspects of the problem that present the function of the concept of cause. In connection with this problem, I think it necessary to consider the question: is cause essential for explanation and prediction? If so, what would be the nature of the causal explanation? Next, we move on to a closer consideration of the nature of the concept of cause. This will finally lead us to the problem of determining the nature of the principle of causality.

1. What is Explanation?

The aim of scientific research is not only to discover and describe social and natural phenomena but also—and more importantly—to explain why these phenomena occur as they do. To explain the phenomena of the physical world and answer the question "why" is one of the primary objects of the natural sciences. "Explanation" is an ambiguous word. What is expected in a "why" question is intellectual satisfaction of one kind or another, and this can be provided partially or completely in different ways. Also, what gives partial or complete satisfaction to one person may offer little or none whatsoever to a person of a different stage of intellectual development. An explanation has two aspects—explanandum and explanans. Explanandum defines the statement of the problem or phenomenon to be explained; by explanans, we mean the class of all these statements wherefrom the explanandum can be derived. The explanans fall into two sub-classes: one of those contain statements stating specific antecedent conditions; the other is a set of statements expressing general laws or hypotheses. An event can be explained by either subsuming it under or relating it to appropriate general laws. It is often said that events can be explained and predicted only in so far they have repeatable characteristics. The term "event" has various shades of meaning but the term event in which a scientist is interested is said to be explained if it is deducible from certain statements of its initial conditions and a set of laws.

A type of explanation commonly encountered in the natural sciences has the formal structure of a deductive argument in which the explanandum is the logical consequence of the explanatory premises. Accordingly, in an explanation of this type, the premises state the sufficient condition for the truth of the explanandum. This type of explanation has been exclusively studied since ancient times. To ask for an explanation as to why a given patient has suffered from a disease is normally to call neither for the clarification of the term "disease" nor for a listing of the symptoms upon which the medical treatment of the disease is to be based, and not even for a theory of disease but rather for an analysis of those antecedent factors in the situation responsible for the patient's falling ill. Such causal diagnosis is generally taken to be a matter of connecting the event to be explained with other events by means of general principles obtained through experience, though not *demonstrable* on the basis of available information. Hume denied such a necessary connection of matters of fact and held that in causal explanation of any event, there is nothing more involved than contingently connecting it with its antecedent circumstances through principles of conjunction induced from past experience. Modern thinkers have largely upheld the view that explanation of events proceeds by way of trying to connect these events with others through general principles based on, though not demonstrable by, experience. Instead of talking of "the cause philosophically speaking", they have tried to construct causal explanation as a pattern of deductive argument, wherein the premises describe particular conditions and formulate general principles, and the conclusion describes the event or events to be explained. It is true that a deductive explanation is commonly called a "causal explanation" and in this case, the conditions referred to by the singular premises of the explanans may jointly be called a cause of the explanandum. There are, however, deductive explanations in which some of the initial conditions occur later than the explanandum and, in these cases, it would not be proper to call the former a cause of the latter. The modern reconstruction of causal explanation as a form of deductive argument has been defended, among others, by Popper and Hempel.

Karl Popper suggests that to offer a causal explanation of an event is to deduce a statement which describes it, using as premises of the deduction one or more universal laws, together with certain singular statements. For instance, we can say that we have given a causal explanation of the breaking of a certain piece of thread if we have found that the thread has a tensile strength of 1 lb and that the weight of 2 lbs was put on it. If we analyse this situation, we find several constituent parts. On the one hand, there is the hypothesis, "whenever a thread is loaded with a weight of exceeding that which characterizes the tensile strength of the thread then it will break." This statement has the character of universal laws of nature. On the other hand, we have singular statements which apply to only the specific event in question: "the weight characteristic for this thread is 1 lb and the weight put on this thread was 2 lbs." It is from this universal statement in conjunction with the statement of initial conditions that we deduce the particular statement "this thread will break".[1] Thus, Popper considers the statements both of universal laws and initial conditions to be "necessary ingredients of a complete causal explanation". The *initial conditions* describe what is usually called the "Cause" of the event *in question*, i.e. the fact that placing a load of 2 lbs on a thread with a tensile strength of 1 lb was the "cause" of its breaking and the prediction describes what is usually called the "effect", i.e. this thread will break. Hempel's account in "The Function of General Laws in History" is similar in this regard. Hempel is of the opinion that the explanation of an event of some specific kind A at a certain place and time indicates the causes or the determining factors of A. Furthermore, the assertion that a set of events have caused the event amounts to the statement that in accordance with certain general laws, a set of events is *regularly followed* by an event of the kind A. Thus, the scientific explanation of an event implies three steps of the process of explanation. These steps: are (i) a set of statements asserting the occurrence of certain events at certain times and places; (ii) a set of universal hypotheses that the statements of both groups are well confirmed by empirical evidence and from the statement of two groups; and (iii) the occurrence of any event can be logically deduced. An explanation of a particular event is often correctly conceived by specifying its *cause* or *causes*. In connection with this problem, Mill states that "An individual fact is said to be explained by pointing out its cause, i.e. by stating the law or laws of causation of which its production is an instance".[2] The causal explanation implicitly claims that there are general laws, $L_1, L_2.............L_n$, in terms of which the causal antecedents of the event to be explained could be regarded as necessary and sufficient conditions for the occurrence of the latter. To argue thus is to claim that the relation between the causal factors and effect is deductive nomological in character. It is a sort of deductive subsumption under principles or general laws. But the converse does not hold good, for there are deductive nomological explanations which would not normally be counted as causal.

The logical structure of a scientific explanation shows that to explain an event is to deduce the explanandum as a consequence of a set of explanans possessing greater generality. But, logic is not sufficient to account for the entire story of knowledge situation. The deductive pattern of explanation also increases our knowledge in the sense that the fact to be explained was not explicitly contained in its class from the beginning. Epistemically, explanation consists in a synthetic or a constructive operation and not merely a deduction of a fact out of a given class. A scientific explanation is free from objectionable circularity if it helps to connect hitherto unconnected specific facts, while the deductive part of the hypothetico-deductive procedure may be said to be "tautological" or "analytic" (in the sense that the *denial* of the conclusion strictly implies the denial of at least one of the premises) but it is not circular (in the sense that the conclusion itself is the sole basis of the inductive probability of the law-like premise). The important point is that a scientific explanation, in order to be regarded as causal, must contain a causal law in it. The essence of a causal explanation consists in having at least one causal law among the class of its major explanans. Also, to test whether a generalization is causal or not, prediction is called for. One important corollary of the deductive pattern of explanation is the thesis that explanation and prediction share an identical logical structure. The structure of a deductive explanation and prediction conforms to what is now called the covering-law-model.[3] This model consists of the deduction of whatever is being explained or predicted from general laws in conjunction with any information about particular facts. In empirical science prediction consists in deriving a statement about a certain future event from: (1) statements describing certain known conditions; and (2) suitable general laws. Thus, a predictive argument can be construed as a deductive argument of the following form:

$$\begin{array}{l} \text{Predictors } L_1, L_2, L_3\ldots\ldots..L_n \\ \text{Explanans } C_1, C_2, C_3\ldots\ldots..C_n \\ \text{Predicted (Explanandum) } \therefore \text{ E} \end{array}$$

On this formulation, L_1, L_2, L_3........L_n are general laws and C_1,C_2,C_3........C_n are statements expressing particular occurrences. Jointly, these premises form the explanans and the conclusion E is the explanandum or statement of the predicted event. Since the explanans logically imply the occurrence of the explanandum, we may assert that the explanans can be used to predict the explanandum if the laws and the particular occurrences adduced in its explanans have been taken into account at a suitable earlier time. The predicted argument of the form has been defined by Hempel as a deductive-nomological prediction. Also, the customary distinction between prediction and explanation, as Hempel thinks,[4] is based upon a pragmatic consideration. Hempel would be inclined to say that in an explanation of the deductive-nomological variety the explanandum which may be past, present or future is taken to be "given" and a set of laws and particular statements is then adduced, which provides premises in an appropriate argument of this type,

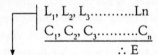

$$\begin{array}{l} L_1, L_2, L_3\ldots\ldots..Ln \\ C_1, C_2, C_3\ldots\ldots..C_n \\ \therefore \text{ E} \end{array}$$

conclusion/deduction/prediction/post-diction

whereas in the case of prediction, the premises are taken to be "given" and the argument then yields a conclusion that an event conforms the pattern of the predictive inference. This characteristic makes explanation and prediction mutually exclusive, although they sometimes coincide. But the thesis of the identification of explanation with prediction is subject to certain critical reflections. Any scientific explanation may be oriented towards the past, while prediction is always oriented towards the future and before we can decide whether explanation and prediction have the same logical structure, we have to ascribe whether the natural laws of our world do, in fact, permit inferences from the present to the future as well as from the present to the past. It is possible that a set of laws governing a given system should permit unique deductive predictions of later states from the given ones, and yet not yield unique deductive retrodictions concerning the earlier states; conversely, a set of laws may permit unique retrodictions but no unique predictions. But this theory is by no means the same as to say that such laws, while permitting an explanation, do not permit prediction. The laws which make predictive argument possible may as well be used for future explanatory purposes. Although these laws permit unique predictions, they do not always permit unique retrodictions. Thus, the objection under consideration misses its point because it tacitly confounds explanation with retrodiction. In an article, Scheffler has subjected the idea of the structural identity of explanation and prediction to a critical scrutiny.[5] He holds that a scientific predictive statement may be false, whereas no explanation is false. This remark is interesting but not correct, for every scientific explanation is open to test or questions. On this assumption, we cannot distinguish an explanation from a prediction. Our suggestion is not that there is a basic discrepancy between explanation and prediction but that the requirement of truth for scientific explanation is restrictive. Explanation, being general, may accommodate the logic of prediction within its fold but it has to be borne in mind that every prediction is not explanatory. There are trivial predictions—too trivial to be regarded as explanations. Certainly there are cases where we can successfully predict some particular phenomenon but cannot provide any explanation for it. Suppose we find that whenever cows lie down in the open fields during the daytime, it is followed up by rains within hours. In such cases, we are in an excellent position for prediction, but scarcely could we offer explanation of the latter in terms of the former. It appears that explanation requires something more than prediction and, to this point, scriven's[6] suggestion is such that the understanding of a phenomenon often enables us to forecast it, the ability to forecast it does not constitute an understanding of a phenomenon. Of course, there is a distinction between explanation and prediction. But before making such a distinction, we should be aware of the distinction between scientific predictions and forecast. Popular prophecies do not depend on laws whereas scientific predictions do. Hence, the differences are much less important than the similarities in the cases of both scientific prediction and scientific explanation. In effect, we are in both cases providing a series of comprehensible statements that have a wide range of logical relations to other statements.

The above considerations may shed some light on the relationship of scientific explanation with prediction. An explanatory argument is also a predictive one. In predicting something as yet unknown, one deductively infers it from particular facts and relevant laws. But can it be held with equal plausibility that a predictive argument always offers a potential explanation? In the case of a deductive nomological prediction, an affirmative answer can be produced. But there are certain sound predictive arguments of the non-deductive type as well which cannot be used as affording potential explanation. It is because of the absence of general laws in the structure of those arguments that they cannot play the role of an explanation. It is the characteristic of explanation—though not necessarily of all predictions—that it presents the inferred phenomena as occurring in conformity with general laws.

Let us admit for the moment that "deduction" is in the very core of the meaning of scientific explanation. Physics is acknowledged to be the most advanced science, for its theories, explanatory and predictive are put forward in the most rigorous objective form. Still, there exists a problem: why must an explanation of events in science be deductive? It is at times claimed that no science really answers the questions as to why any event occurs at all and why things are related in certain ways and not otherwise. Such questions could be answered only if we were able to prove that the events which occur must occur and the relations that hold between things must do so. For this purpose, the necessary and sufficient reason for the occurrences have to be shown. It is also thought that the task of a natural science is to conceptually describe the sequence of observable events and that natural science cannot explain or account for the existence of such occurrences. Science, therefore, presents only what is comprehensible or conceptual description, and not explanation. But this again is questionable because the argument assumes that there is just one correct sense in which "why" questions can be raised, namely the sense in which the proper answer to it is a *proof* of the *inherent necessity* of the proposition. There are, in fact, well-established uses for the words "why" and "explanation" so that it is entirely appropriate to designate an answer to a "why" question as an explanation even when the reply does not supply reasons for regarding the explanandum as intrinsically necessary. Although the universality of the deductive pattern is open to objections, it is hardly disputable that many explanations in the sciences and most comprehensive systems of explanations are of this form. But why is it so? If the generalizations and individual statements of fact are accepted as true, then because of the essential relation, the connection must also be true. This is the virtue of a deductive model of explanation. Once such terms as "must", "guarantees" are clarified, then it becomes understandable as to why deduction alone justifies conclusion. And, since this deduction in most cases uses causal laws in order to deduce the conclusion, so in most cases this deduction assumes a model of explanation that is inevitably causal and also shares the same logical structure as that of prediction.

Causal explanation, considered as answers to the question, "why" gives rise to various complications. It is not expected to be answered by detailing all the events which make up a total cause. The formal explanation would be to produce the necessary and sufficient conditions for the explanandum. A fact conceived to be indispensable for the origination of another is also regarded as a cause in respect of the latter. A cause in science is the minimum conditions required to satisfactorily account for any example of an observable effect. A causal condition of any event is any condition which had it not occurred, given only those other conditions the event itself would not have occurred. If this is so then it at once follows that the cause, that is the totality of those necessary conditions, is also sufficient for the occurrence of the event in question. Once all the conditions necessary for the occurrence of the given event have been enumerated, the totality of conditions will immediately be sufficient for its occurrence or such that no further conditions will be necessary. When a given set of conditions is sufficient for the occurrence of a given event, it would mean that those conditions were such that when all of them occurred, the effect in question could not fail to occur. Thus, an explanation in terms of a cause requires an answer which is both one of a set of events which together form a sufficient condition and one which in the presence of the rest of the set of events is a necessary condition. We express these necessary and sufficient conditions in the form of the premises of a causal explanation.

If, by the word "cause", we mean that which makes the occurrence of a thing intelligible or that which is necessary and sufficient for the occurrence of an event, then it can be unhesitatingly claimed that it is essential for some cases of deductive pattern of explanation. Predictability is not necessarily the meaning of causality; it is a criterion of causal as well as non-causal determination. Identifying explanation with prediction, we ignore the fact that explanation and prediction are two separate activities involving two different kinds of knowledge. Significant predictions may not contain explanatory force. Similarly, explanatory argument may not have a predictive ability. A predictive argument can be and is construed scientifically in a deductive model so a deductive model, in most cases, leads to a causal model. In effect, it would not be unfair to say that the identical relation between explanation and prediction ultimately rests upon a serious confusion.

2. Causal Explanation and Functional Explanation

An explanation of an event in terms of its cause remains incomplete unless we compare it with an explanation in terms of its function. The word "function" is highly ambiguous. Different interpretations of the term are possible. Functional explanation, as considered by Nagel,[7] possesses two forms. It may be sought for a particular act, state or thing at a stated time, e.g. the functional answer to the question as to why I am staying in Kolkata all through October—that I am doing so in order to complete my paper. Or, a functional explanation may be offered for a feature that is present in all systems of a certain kind, at whatever time such a system may exist, e.g. the presence of lungs in the human body is explained by showing that they operate in a stated manner *in order to* maintain a chemical process and thereby to assume continuance of life for the body into the future. Since in the functional explanation of lungs there is no such assumption that the lungs have any conscious end-in-view, it is not necessarily an indication of anthropomorphism. In the first formulation of functional explanation, it is suggested by Nagel that "why" questions about a particular activity are answered by specifying a goal or end towards the attainment of which the activity is a means. This view is shared, among others, by Braithwaite.[8] If, by explanation in terms of function is taken to be an explanation in terms of purpose, then it is a perfectly acceptable first stage explanation. But here the interesting point is that this account of functional explanation should not be confused with what is referred to as causal explanation.

Secondly, functional explanation, as understood by modern mathematicians, is altogether different from the account already offered. To signify the relation of dependence or interdependence between two or more variable factors—whether these factors are measurable or not—is to explain anything functionally. This pattern of explanation may be expressed by stating that the suicide rate in a community is a function of the degree of social cohesion achieved by it. Functional explanation is indicative of the functional relation obtained between two such classes as that for every member of one of the classes there is at least a member of the other class. A question which seems to have remained yet unanswered is: are causal explanations and functional explanations identical? A plausible answer may be found along the following lines:

(1) On the first formulation of functional explanation, it does not assume that the unrealized future state caused people to be engaged in certain activities, though it definitely states that such a goal prompted or motivated people to be engaged so. Hence, it would be unreasonable to think that the future acts causally on the present. It is equally meaningless to talk of future oxidation of foods in the body, bringing about lungs into existence. In effect, functional explanation should not be confused with explanation in terms of cause. It is equally objectionable to regard that the existing desire for a certain kind of future causes people to act in certain ways. No amount of reasoning is sufficient to prove that man's *desire* can *serve* as *causes*.

(2) On modern empiricists' assumption, functional relation helps us to predict the unobserved event from the observed ones. Since the predictability of unobserved event by means of observed ones is the central problem of causality, so causal relation is and can be defined with the help of functional relation. Bertrand Russell[9] shares this view when he says that causal laws state a functional relation between certain events at a certain time and other events at earlier or later times. It is undoubtedly true that functional laws are the laws of probability. Sometimes it is thought that probabilistic explanations are only a halfway house to the deductive model. Here, it is necessary

to replace the statistical assumptions in the premises of probabilistic explanations by a strictly universal statement. Actually, it is a difficult task. It is a big mistake to confuse the causal or deductive pattern of explanation with the probabilistic pattern of the same. The distinction between the two is to be traced to the difference in the logical relation between explanans and explanandum. In the probabilistic pattern, the relation between the two is only probable, while in the (deductive) causal pattern, it cannot be so. If by "cause" is meant necessary and sufficient conditions for the occurrence or production of an event or a thing, then it would be quite in order to characterize the relation between the explanans and the explanandum of causal inference as "necessary". Further, such a characterization becomes possible if we could show that the framing of a causal hypothesis is of a different sort of a thing. I propose to clarify the issue in the following chapter.

The above analysis makes it abundantly clear as to why causal explanation should not be confused with functional explanation. In the Aristotelian scheme of science, no explanation is admissible which does not refer to a telos or purpose. What Aristotle means is this: every causal explanation, on analysis, turns out to be teleological. But modern science regards final causes as too pure to be of any relevance to the study of physical and chemical processes. Hence, this reduction seems to be unreasonable. Finally, it seems that explanation of "natural events" is essentially of the "deductive model", i.e. of the causal model, and that of "human actions" is to be organized in teleological or functional, i.e. non-deductive model. In other words, teleological explanations of "natural events" and causal explanations of "human actions" have no scientific standing or logical basis. Consequently, I do not deny—or perhaps nobody would—that causes are—necessary for explanation and prediction (as we have tried to prove earlier) of natural events. But what precisely is the concept of "cause"? This is what I would like to analyse in the following section.

3. What is Cause?

A cause in science is the minimum conditions required to satisfactorily account for any example of an observed result. There seems to be a need to distinguish the causal conditions from the other conditions, given which, certain changes occur. The causal conditions of any change are, in some cases, necessary for its occurrence. In other words, these conditions are such that had any of them not occurred, the change in question would not have happened at all. The kind of necessity involved here is not logical necessity, since there is never any logical contradiction in affirming that one change occurred and the other did not. The rejection of the claim of logical necessity introduces us to accept certain concepts such as physical, nomological, etc. A causal condition of any event is any condition which had it not occurred, given only those other conditions, the event would not have occurred. If this is so then it at once follows that the cause—that is the totality of those necessary conditions—is also sufficient for the occurrence of the event in question. Once an individual has enumerated all the conditions necessary for the occurrence of the given event, the totality of conditions will at once be sufficient for its occurrence or there might be a situation that no further conditions will be necessary. If a given set of conditions was sufficient for the occurrence of a given event, it would mean that those conditions were such that when all of them occurred, the effect in question could not fail to occur. Someone might object to this theory that to state that a cause is always a sufficient as also a necessary condition is dogmatic and semantically naive. This is so, because a person can never discover a sufficient condition for a given event in the sense that he can never be *absolutely* certain that our prediction of the effect will be *completely* verified. This is, in fact, an important objection, but it loses much of its importance because the demand for *absolute* certainty is a hopeless quest on the part of a finite man and it would be more reasonable to regard that a person can discover such a state of affairs which would be necessary and sufficient for a given event. In other words, given the conditions under which the effect may take place, the person's prediction of the effect is or could be tested. Therefore, the condition depending upon which a fact arises is a causal condition. A fact which is conceived to be indispensable for the origination of another is also to be regarded as a cause in respect of the latter. It was discovered long ago that only a combination of several factors gives rise to an effect, which again, is a complex of several other factors. It is never found that one single unaided event—however important and outstanding it is—is capable of producing another event as its effect. It should, therefore, be borne in mind that a cause is always a combination of conditions. It is for the sake of convenience that the causal relation is stressed between two individual events. But this is only a methodological device and should not be interpreted as an exhaustive ontological analysis.

Any adequate analysis of a causal relation presupposes four aspects, viz., continuity, difference, absence of activity and determination. The non-recognition of continuity leads to some undesirable consequences. How can the causal relation to be possibly explained unless some contact is supposed to exist between the cause and the effect, i.e. the earlier and the later event, both in time and space? Secondly, in philosophy, it was taken for granted that the difference between a cause and its effect was one of power, or that a cause acts upon its effect in a manner in which the effect does not act upon the cause. Modern philosophers, on the other hand, have for the most part tried to distinguish the causes from the effects in terms of temporal considerations. Most philosophers have supposed that causes should be distinguished from their effects in terms of time, and if that is done, there is no need to speak of any special power of the cause in relation to its effect. But it has lately been doubted whether an analytic distinction between causes and effects can be drawn without any reference to such notion as power or efficacy as to why a cause might not follow its effect in time. Why should A be considered the cause rather than the effect of B? It is only the element of efficacy that distinguishes causes from effects and this cannot be *shown* empirically. The idea of a causal power is perhaps esoteric; yet there is no obvious way of eliminating it from the concept of causation. The concept of power is highly controversial. This concept is bound to remind one of Hume's observations. Hume is of opinion that mental happenings produce the idea of power. We ascribe to objects an additional property of power, efficacy or causal necessity but we get the idea of that power only from what we feel internally in contemplating the objects around us. Terms such as "power", "efficacy" and "production" are nearly synonymous. Hume rejects all the vulgar definitions that provide no real explanation of the content of the idea. Against Hume, it can be argued that human knowledge is not to be necessarily defined by the bounds of senses alone because the reach of our senses is very limited. Thus, a Humean analysis cannot provide a sufficient ground for the denial of the concept of power.

In Indian philosophy, it is Mīmāṃsāka who accepts power or potentiality to be a distinct category on par with things or realities. The prevailing Nyāya view is that causal power does not form a separate category. Our verbal usage is based on the notion of power. In this connection, it is interesting to note the views of R. Harré and E.I. Madden whose opinion is that the concept of power is neither magical nor occult. It is an empirical concept. In spite of their different opinions, one thing that is to be noted in this connection is that all of them agree in favour of this concept. In effect, we can unhesitatingly state that the concept of power is an intrinsic vital concept and it is closely associated with the concept of cause and so on. Thirdly, causality has nothing to do with the exercise of activity. It cannot be supposed that a cause consciously exerts an activity with a view to the production of the effect. It only presupposes that a preceding event is, by its natural constitution, productive of the subsequent event and this is confirmed by the uniformity of the succession of the two events in all circumstances. Finally, the specific nature of the cause and the effect presupposes a relation of entailment (physical). A specific cause produces a specific effect. The fallacy of the doctrine of non-causality is an upshot of the doctrine of non-recognition of the peculiarity of the connection obtained between what we call cause and effect. This connection is absent between events related otherwise. All connections are not obviously causal.

4. Cognitive Status of Cause

A discussion of the causal relation remains incomplete unless something is said about the cognitive status of cause. The cognitive status of cause in general has been the subject of a long and inconclusive debate. In order to clarify the issue, I concentrate upon some well-known classical views as well as some contemporary trends of thought. On the question of the cognitive status of cause, I propose to confine myself to the examination of the following two positions.

> (1) cause is "objective"
> (2) cause is "subjective"

The first position maintains that a cause always points to a real world, while the second position maintains that a cause is always "internal" and is the play of inner sense. To clarify the position, the following questions are to be answered:

(a) Is cause "objectively necessary"?
(a¹) Is cause "objectively contingent?
(b) Is cause "subjectively necessary"?
(b¹) Is cause "subjectively contingent"?

(a) The expression "objectively necessary" stands for the view that the necessary connection which constitutes the meaning of the word "cause", is not a mere form of the human mind, i.e. in reality everything necessitates everything else. This view has been found in the works of Aristotle, Spinoza and some other philosophers.

(a¹) The expression "objectively contingent" indicates that the causal construction of the world is essentially contingent. This view has been recognized, among others, by Russell and Broad.

(b) The third position, i.e. "subjectively necessary" means that necessity is not in the world out there; in space; its origin is to be discovered in the structure of human mind itself. This is an anti-skeptic phenomenalist view advocated by Kant and his followers. Its pro-skeptic version has been defended by the Humeans.

(b¹) The fourth position, viz., the subjective contingency of cause lies in thinking that causal regularity is only a way of our looking at things. This view may be attributed to Woodger. Hume's name has also been often mentioned in this connection.

(a) Let us first consider the view of Aristotle. To know is to know by means of causes—this is the gist of Aristotle's teaching[10]. Aristotle offers, as we all know, a fourfold classification of cause, viz., material, formal, efficient and final which are jointly necessary and sufficient for the production of its effect. His notion of the relation between a cause and its effect can be formulated in at least three different ways; but on analysis it is found that they are all the variations of the same necessarian view of causality.

(1) A cause is that which explains the effect.

(2) A cause is that which makes intelligible the occurrence of the effect

(3) A cause is that whose knowledge is necessary for the knowledge of the thing.

The above three formulations are based on the fact that the knowledge of a thing is necessarily the knowledge of its causes. But some remarks may be made against this view. A cause is not necessary in the sense that causal explanation of a thing exhausts all the possible forms of its explanation. Causal explanation is, at best, an important form of explanation of the nature of a thing. Further, Aristotle's introduction to fourfold classification of causes cannot account for that sort of necessary connection between a cause and its effect, as Aristotle imagined. Aristotle thought that natural philosophers must take into account of each of the four causes and refer to them all in explaining events. But the underlying intention of Aristotle's notions of efficient cause and final cause was to prove the teleological character of nature. It means that natural events are all drawn towards an end and intrinsically connected with it. We accept that causes are necessary even for the explanation of human actions but human actions are not caused in the way (one-one relation) natural events are. The denial of the doctrine of the one-one relation between a cause and its effect is inconsistent with Aristotle's general metaphysical principle. Aristotle's classification seems to destroy the autonomy of science by subordinating material, efficient causes to final causes. If the word "cause" is taken to mean that which is *necessary* and *sufficient* for the occurrence of a thing, then no purpose or ideal or end can properly account for this. Secondly, Aristotle's formulation of the objectivity of cause follows from the fact that cause constitutes the form or structure of nature; nature is essentially causal. But what is meant by nature? In Aristotle's analysis, nature means two things: the matter and the form of which the latter is the end. Since all the rest is for the sake of an end, the form must be the sense of "that for the sake of which". The matter must be there because the form requires it for its realization. Aristotle's notion of nature was different from the modern scientists'. The world of natural events does not necessarily presuppose the idea of design, as Aristotle thought. Search for a telos or a final cause, which transcends the boundaries of the world of natural events, would be a baffled search as human understanding would always be determined by the spatio-temporal situation and influenced by other particular and variable subjective conditions. Simply put, it is not a "failure" on the part of the scientists to properly appreciate the nature of a telos which is driving the world towards itself. Rather, it would be proper for scientific explanation to do without transcendent causes. Hence, Aristotle's notion of the objectivity of cause presupposed such an idea of nature, which is very different from nature as ordinarily conceived by the scientist.

A rigid formulation of the objective necessity of cause is also found in the philosophy of Spinoza,[11] for example. The word "cause", as it is generally used in Spinoza's philosophy, is anything that explains the existence or qualities of the effect. For Spinoza, to explain means to show that one true proposition is the logical consequence of some other; explanation essentially involves exhibiting the "necessary connection" and the phrase "necessary connection" in this context means a strictly logical connection to be discovered by the logical analysis of the ideas involved. Causation is purely a logical relation of ground and consequent. Causal laws are the necessary presuppositions of God's essential nature. Spinozistic analysis settles the fact that all explanations essentially involve reference to causes which are necessarily connected with its effect but this necessity is not open to any further modifications. The question, however, remains: how can an imperfect, finite, temporal being possibly claim deductive necessity for natural events unless he possesses a third eye? Spinoza's formulation of necessity is inconsistent with the finitude and temporal character of man, and therefore, purely speculative in nature. Secondly, to think that reality has a necessary causal structure is to think that necessity defines the very structure of reality or nature, which in Spinoza's terminology, is identical with God. But the attempt to identify with the all-inclusive (conscious) totality or God is to make an assumption without offering any empirical correlate. So, this idea of objectivity is untenable. Since the attempt undertaken by Aristotle and Spinoza is purely speculative and not empirically adequate, it is hardly defensible.

(a)[1] Let us now pass on to the second position which characterizes cause as objectively contingent. Russell's view[12] regarding the contingency of causation stems from his general doctrine that the strict, certain and universal law of causation—which some philosophers advocate as an ideal—may possibly be true but not known to be true in the light of any available evidence. Although Russell has not spoken of causes but his examination of "causal laws" covers "causes". The approximate uniformities which lead to its pre-scientific employment may turn out to be true in all but a few very rare and exceptional circumstances. In such cases, it is convenient to be able to speak of the antetcedent event as the "cause" and the consequent event as the "effect". It is in this sense that Russell intends to use these words. Any constant relation between the events of a specified kind with given intervals of time between them is a "causal law". Russell's formulation of the causal concept, in essence, conforms to the theory of uniform sequence. The attempt to give meaning to the concept of cause in terms of the regularity of sequence is an endeavour to vindicate the thesis that causal laws are to be construed empirically, i.e. contingently. Necessity is on Russell's interpretation, a predicate of a propositional function, i.e. it is necessary for all possible values of its arguments. Russell's formula of causation does not appear to be an adequate conceptual reconstruction of the causal bond. What it can say at best is this: the cause and effect are regularly associated. Russell is of the opinion that causal relation obtains in between things or events. A cause is an event or group of events of some known general character and possessing a known relation to some other event called the effect. According to Russell, a physical event is an event which is *inferred* and which is not known to be mental while a mental event is an event which is known without inference. Russell holds the view that the knowledge of the physical object is obtained through an acquaintance with the sense data and it is not a direct knowledge. He also says that the knowledge of the physical event is what he calls "knowledge by description."[13] The real physical object is not immediately known to us at all, but must be an inference from what is *immediately* known. Now, whatever be the nature of physical event, this much perhaps we can clarify since causes, according to Russell, are the character of *things* and not of *thoughts*, they are objective. But this account of objectivity is based upon such a conception of events that it can hardly be regarded as consistent with realism or descriptivism. It is no wonder that Russell's theory of description, instead of strengthening the cause of realism, in fact, weakens it. It is a step towards phenomenalism or constructionism. It is not correct to think that we infer or construct physical events;

rather, we discover them. What *produces* and what is *produced* are always events but it would be a mistake to think that we are the producer of "what is produced" and "what produces".

Like Russell, Broad also thinks[14] that a causal relation is a contingent relation and the generation of the physical event is more of the causal type. Broad's account of contingency of the causal relation follows from the fact that though—given the structure of the actual—a thing would not have one kind of mass without having another, there might still be a world in which the one appeared without the other. But Broad differs from Russell in holding that causation does not mean any kind of regular sequence. It is true that certain kinds of regular sequence are fairly trustworthy signs of the presence of causal relation. The missing factor seems to be certain spatio-temporal continuity between the sequent events. For P does not cause Q in spite of the complete regularity between the two. Broad is correct in supposing that the empirical sign for causal relation is the uniformity of sequence but he is wrong in assuming that mere uniformity of sequence plus spatio-temporal continuity can account for such a causal relation. To this, the notion of productivity should be added. Broad is perhaps not prepared to properly accommodate such an idea in his scheme of thought. Broad's analysis presupposes that an event is a particular existence and the production of any event is the production of a new particular. When one event generates another, we call the former cause and the latter effect. But what about this generation? Surely, Broad cannot offer any empirical demonstration of this process of generation. Furthermore, since causal relations have a definite location in space-time and since space-time are real objects of the world, causes are always objective. But the point which appears objectionable to us may be stated thus: that which is purely particular cannot be identified at all and fruitfully enquired into. A sequence between two particulars cannot be characterized as a case of causation unless it is simultaneously a case of invariable relation between the universals by which the particulars are characterized.

(b) The inadequacy of the Russell-Broad interpretation of cause as objectively contingent leads us to consider the third alternative, which states that causes are subjectively necessary. This view has been developed by Hume and improved upon and defended by Kant, although their interpretations, as we all know, are inherently different. The relation of cause and effect is of interest to Hume[15] because he regards it as the foundation of all factual reasoning, and necessary connection is the defining characteristic of a causal relation. But the source from which the idea of necessary connection is supposed to be derived is completely non-demonstrable. Hume's account of necessity can be characterized as subjective in the sense that the "necessity" characterizing the relation of the events does not reside in the objective relation of the events themselves. The necessity has its locus elsewhere—in certain habits of expectation developed in the human mind as a result of the uniform but *de-facto* conjunction of events. There is nothing in the object to compel us to believe that they are necessarily connected. The ground of causal necessity is certain dispositions of our mind. Events are entirely loose and separate; they are conjoined but never connected. We habitually ascribe an objectively necessary connection to a subjectively felt necessity. People can very well conceive of a change in the course of nature without necessarily thinking of a causal connection and this does not involve any contradiction.

But Hume's analysis has been questioned on the grounds that an ability to conceive the contradictory of a supposed necessity does not prove that actually there is no necessity. If physical necessity is all that we mean, then there is nothing wrong in thinking that causality can be characterized by the same. For Hume, the proposition "A caused B" is based on the sense-impressions of the two events A and B: whenever a sense impression of an event like A occurs, it is immediately followed by a sense-impression of an event such as B. Hume identifies this feeling with the impression of causal necessity which is produced "inside the mind" by the association of ideas. Hume's analysis of necessary connection begins with the assumption that there is a universal correspondence between impressions and ideas. But his search for an impression from which this idea might be derived is something really queer. This point has been raised by Kneale. By the word "impression," Hume means what modern philosophers call a sensum, e.g. a flash, a noise, etc., and an idea is an image. Hume fails to see that it is possible to think of a necessary connection but certainly it cannot be imagined; there is no reason to suppose that it must be *sensible* because it is *thinkable*. Hume's view of universal correspondence between impressions and ideas prepares the ground for the denial of the doctrine of causal necessity. That causal laws are not confined to our experience was not duly noted by Hume. Failure of our causal predictions does not prove that the concerned laws are subjective. Reflection on the "subjective" necessity discloses its objective foundation. And this is the main point that Kant argrues[16] so elaborately and carefully against Hume. He says that if we want to distinguish the objective succession of events in the phenomenal world from the subjectivity of our ideas, we must regard the former succession as necessarily determined and governed by the rule of cause and effect. The proof Kant offered by in defending this rule provides his answer to Hume's critique of causal relation. The main point in the controversy seems to be that succession in the object can only be understood as causally connected. It is incorrect to think that by cause Kant means nothing more than regular sequence. The necessity which Kant attributes to the subjective order of our sense-impressions is not known by observation but is a consequence of its derivation from an objective order. For Kant, necessity is never empirical; it cannot be ascertained by observation. It is, rather, a necessary precondition of intelligible organization of what we observe. Necessity iş in accordance with rule. The "first" event having been given, in accordance with such a rule, we must go on to apprehend the "second" event. The necessary connection is the relation of cause and effect. And this constitutes the ground for Kant's necessarian view of causality. The necessary character of causal relation is to be found in the structure of understanding. The understanding which makes experience not only possible but also intelligible by its causal synthesis cannot itself be derived from experiences. The reason as to why the causal connection prevails throughout this objective world as known to us is that this world consists only of appearances, and that the mind must posit appearances in one common homogenous time. To do this is to subject appearances to the rule of causality; for without this, the unity of time and thus the unity of apperception would disappear, and there could be no experience, no objective world. This analysis persuades us to believe that necessity is in the human mind. Apart from its relation to human mind, the world has no causal structure. It is understanding which imposes causes upon the facts of experience. This is phenomenalism, pointing out the relativity of knowledge, the dependence of the phenomenal world of objects upon the mind, and indicating thereby the impossibility of knowing the real. The affections of sensibility are purely subjective and there can be no necessity in sense-manifolds and it is human mind as a knower projects in necessitating them. Causes, according to Kant, are only "in us". Kant might also claim that objectivity resides in categorical experience. It is true that man is not free enough to categorize his experiences in whatever way he likes; still there is an important point in asserting that causal experience is subjective. Kant's concept of causal necessity may be objected to on the ground that by making the world of sense-manifolds blind, he tries to underestimate the powers and the capacities of the world of objects. To credit thought with the powers of both making the world possible and also of testing it unilaterally is to deny the critical and growing character of human knowledge. One might say that the Kantian knowledge and knowledge-making apparatus never encounter an unkantian world, which is strange. It clearly defeats the very critical power of Kant's philosophy. Our primary interest, however, is to show that both Hume and Kant have offered subjective interpretations of cause. Both of them agree in holding that causal necessity is a kind of mental determination. There is nothing in the world (which according to Hume is the world of sense-impression and which for Kant is the world of sense-experience) to inform us about causal necessity although they differ deeply so far as their idea of nature or world is concerned. What differentiates Hume's theory from Kant is this: the former confesses the skeptical character of mental determination, and the latter affirmed the *infallible* character of the same. In spite of this, difference, both of them have attempted to preserve the subjective notion of necessity which is inconsistent with realism.

(b¹) Let us now consider the last but an important alternative which states that cause is always contingent and exists only in us. This position is advocated by Woodger[17] who is of the opinion that the notion of causes arises when we find that changes of one thing are regularly related to changes in another. Woodger's central thesis states that since causal nexus is not observable, causal relation is contingent. We agree with the author that causal nexus is not observable but not with the views that its contingency is dependent thereupon. The verifiable content of a concept should not be confused with its meaning-content. Woodger's account of subjectivity follows from his assumption that causes do not constitute the structure of the world. No event of nature as such is either a cause or an effect. The world becomes causal by virtue of its relation to the human mind. But what is to be borne in mind is that there is something in some events because of which we can apply the causal category only to them and not to others. If events do not express themselves as causes, then no amount of reasoning is able to make such a satisfactory distinction between causal and non-causal sorts of determination. Hence, the attempt to interpret causes as subjectively contingents is untenable.

So far I have been arguing to prove that the analysis of the expressions such as "objectively necessary", "subjectively necessary", "objectively contingent", "subjectively contingent", do not adequately reveal the cognitive status of cause. The question remains: what would be the proper way of explaining the true status of cause? Broadly speaking, the answer I suggest is: "objectively necessary". This expression can be attributed to causes provided the words "objective" and "necessity" are understood in the following manner. Causes are objective in the sense that these are *not* a human *construct* but a structural description of natural phenomena. By this we mean that the events themselves possess the powers and properties of showing themselves as causes. To know is to discover or organize experience under appropriate categories. But the conditions of our knowledge are so limited that an infallible description or organization or discovery is not possible. The causal structures of the world are so complex that it is very difficult to be certain that these will be uniformly repeated in the sub-structural levels. Causal necessity, whose empirical schema is the regularity of sequence, is always open to test by prediction. Consequently, it is also relative to certain conditions. Someone might claim contingency for the meaning of the word "necessity". But what we fail to understand is this: mere contingency is not the meaning of the word "causality". If we are right in thinking that strict necessity holds nowhere in nature, then we are allowed to assign a sort of relative necessity to explain the cognitive status of cause. The denial of this sort of necessity miserably fails to explain the *development* of human knowledge. Causal necessity must not be confused with logical necessity. The world has perhaps its ontological causal structures and sub-structures, and as realists we do not deny it. But the interesting point is: we cannot be epistemically too sure about it. That is why, by framing causal hypothesis and testing them in the light of appropriate empirical findings, we try to approximate and truly describe the causal structures and sub-structures of the world.

5. The Nature of the Principle of Causality

"The principle of causality" means that any event whatsoever can be causally explained. Is there anything strange in the claim "Every event has a cause"? It is natural enough that sometimes there should disagreement about the nature of the principle of causality. As to the nature of the principle of causality, the question that might arise is: whether it is necessary or contingent. The necessarian character of the principle has been defended, among others, by Leibnitz and Kant and the empiricists like Hume and Mill have maintained that the principle of causality is contingent.

Leibnitz holds[18] the view that the general principle of causality is itself a truth of reason. On this premise, the causal principle applies and applies *necessarily* to all possible worlds; for if a truth is necessary, everything we conceive under it must be in accordance with it. The principle of causality is thus a *necessary* principle, valid of things in general, and capable of metaphysical as well as empirical use. Although this notion was not explicitly affirmed by other rationalists, it seems to have been widely accepted. But if the principle means that it is always logically possible to construct a causal explanation, then the assertion that any event whatsoever can be causally explained is tautological. For, in every case of prediction, we can find causal laws which make prediction possible. But every explanation is not necessarily a causal explanation and since this principle is open to modification, so it cannot be considered necessary in the rationalist sense.

The viewpoint that every event has a cause embodies a synthetic truth has been a matter of dispute in philosophy. Any disagreement on the point is understandable. Of the statements which are called synthetic, concepts such as "contingent", "factual", "empirical" and "a posteriori" are predicable. Further, to the analytic statements, we apply such predicates as "logically necessary", "true by definition" and "a priori." Here we expect the contradictories to be logically impossible. J.S. Mill[19] is one of those few who maintain that the causal principle is synthetic in nature. Mill proposed to investigate causality as it fell within experience, i.e. a synthetic, a *posteriori* or contingent truth. But the defect in this doctrine is considerable. However much experience we have had of causal sequences in the past, we have no logical right to expect similar successions in the future. For no amount of empirical generalization can give rise to a truly *universal* proposition. Mill is certainly right in his approach to the problem in saying that we must investigate causality as it falls within experience and once we decide to do that, we cannot help believing that causality is a relation involving sequence, or at least order in time and, therefore, applicable only to temporal objects. To apply it to the timeless objects of traditional metaphysics and use it in an unrestricted way are said to be logically impermissible. But, the weakness in Mill's strategy lies in deducing the principle from the facts of experience and to characterize it as contingent.

We must try to make clarify what is or might be involved in the claim that the principle of causality is a synthetic necessary truth. Underlying the view that it is synthetic, there seem to be two main reasons: (1) the statement "Every event has a cause" cannot be plausibly represented as analytic. There is no definition of "event" by means of which "Every event has a cause" can be transformed into a manifest tautology. Since it seems impossible to hold that "Every event has a cause" is analytic, tautologous and true by definition and since the statement "some events have no cause" is not self-contradictory, so it leads us to hold that the principle is synthetic. (2) The principle of causation appears to be a statement about the course of nature—about what actually occurs in the universe. In effect, the principle is to be judged as synthetic. Some consideration may be offered in support of the view that the causal principle is synthetic. To this opinion, one might say that it is impossible to prove that this synthetic principle is also *necessary*. The reason in favour of this argument is that the expression "necessary" means "logically necessary", or that the expression "synthetic necessary" is self-contradictory. But we think that it is not so. There are statements which can be regarded as necessary (e.g. Nothing can be red and green all over) but cannot be shown to be tautologous by the use of formal definitions. Those who regard that the principle of causality is synthetically necessary may mean that what it intends to express must be about the course of nature but it can be accepted as true without any appeal to sense-experience, to start with.

The principle of causality, for Kant, is a synthetic necessary truth[20] Kant thinks that synthetic necessary judgements cannot rest for their validity on sense-experience, since they are necessary and universal. We all know that Kant made an important contribution to the elucidation of this problem and most of us suppose that it offered a refutation to Hume. But this seems to be a highly mistaken idea. The agreement of Hume and Kant is as striking as their difference. Despite his radically empiricist approach Hume does not deny that the principle of causality is valid throughout the domain of sense-experience, while Kant is just as anxious as Hume to argue that the necessity of the causal principle cannot be purely *logical*. Kant based causality on understanding while Hume traced its ground in imagination and the difference between the two is not as sharp as it has often been made out. Kant argued that if we are to distinguish the objective succession of events from the subjective succession of our ideas, we must regard the former succession as necessarily determined by the law of cause and effect. Kant's argument for the objectivity of causality results from the general lines of his theory of objects. The objective is what we necessarily think and objective causal successions are distinguished from other successions by the help of a necessary rule. The necessity which marks a causal relation is accordingly derived from the necessity of the general principle of causality itself. The principle of causality is *necessary* in the sense that it cannot derive its validity from sense-experience alone. Judgements of experience are all synthetic. It would be absurd to try to seek an analytic judgment based on experience. In the statement "Everything which happens has its cause", the concept "cause" lies entirely outside the other concept and indicates something quite different from "that which happens" and is therefore, not, contained in this latter representation. But, how can we apprehend that the concept of cause, though not contained in it, yet belongs and indeed necessarily to it? It cannot be experience, because the suggested principle has connected the second idea with the character of necessity, and therefore, completely *apriori* on the basis of pure concepts. That the possibility of human knowledge *entails* the necessity of the causal principle had been presumed by Kant. Without accepting the detailed philosophical position of Kant, we can agree with him in characterizing the principle of causality as "synthetic necessary". It is one of the misleading assumptions in philosophy that all propositions of the world can be classified either as analytic or synthetic. The distinction becomes significant within the area of certain decisions. It is true that the necessity of the causal principle is followed from its invariability. Kant is advocating for the absolute necessity of the principle but here the important point to note is that it is only in connection with human knowledge that the principle of causality is relatively necessary. Growth of knowledge is indeed a fact. Modifiability of the principle is indicative of its necessary character. Causal organization of human knowledge cannot remain what it is irrespective of the field of its application. In other words, its validity is partly dependent upon the events purported to be connected by it. Therefore, a Kantian attempt to construct the principle of causality as absolutely necessary is not defensible.

We may now raise the question: what is necessary to disprove the thesis that the assertion "Every natural event has a cause"? A verbal answer suggested is "an uncaused event". Hence, arises a difficulty. There cannot be any natural event which could be characterized as uncaused, for an uncaused natural event is unidentifiable and unintelligible. Also, it makes little sense to say that it is natural. Any counter-evidence to the assertion "Every event has a cause" is unavailable as a matter of principle. If necessity is claimed for it solely on the ground that it is completely independent of the actual course of events, the assertion cannot be considered as synthetic. It is in Warnock's terminology "vacuous" rather than necessary. These arguments tend to show that there must be something wrong with the view that the principle of causality expresses a synthetic necessary truth.

The belief in the principle of causality is on Popper's interpretation[21] metaphysical. He does not believe in any sharp line of demarcation between the "empirical" and the "metaphysical", yet he admits at least this much that while empirical or scientific statements are falsifiable, the metaphysical statements are not. If the principle of causality be a metaphysical principle, then it is not capable of being falsified. But we shall try to show that the principle of causality is criticizable or modifiable, though with some difficulty, even if a single counter-evidence to the principle comes to our notice (we would try to show that the principle does not hold good in the realm of mental events and human actions). The fact that the principle of causality is modifiable shows that it is synthetic or informative in the weak sense. The sense in which the principle of causality is informative is not the same in which the particular causal laws are. The principle of causality does not directly pass a judgment of experience. This principle is informative in the sense that it has a domain of its application. Consequently, its character can be satisfactorily described by treating it as a recommendation, a presupposition. It is a presupposition in connection with the domain of its application. Every natural event starts with the idea that the events of the world can be causally related and explained. In the case of a particular causal law, the finding of a single variation of the law would render the law falsified, whereas in the case of a general principle, the discovery of a single variation although difficult—in principle not impossible—would render the principle modified. If this line of reasoning is tenable, then there is no good reason why we should not reject the contention that the principle of causality is not synthetic. We have found it impossible to defend the strict sense of "necessity" in the natural world, so it would not be wrong to attribute a sort of relative necessity to this principle.

CHAPTER II

The Analysis of Causal Laws

In this chapter, my main task is to examine the character of causal laws. This is so, because we cannot analyze an event causally unless we assume some causal law or laws. The attempts to define causal laws in terms of the counter-factuals have not proved to be successful. It is true that laws have the form of universal conditionals. To say that a universal statement can be shown to be lawlike if and only if it is seen to sustain its corresponding "counterfactual", and to say that the rationality of a counter-factual is constituted by its deducibility from its corresponding universal is to say the same thing from two different ends, or argue in a circle. The value of a contrary-to-fact conditional as a criterion of distinction between a "connected" and an "accidental" universal is open to doubt. This view has been defended by Popper[22] also and without going into the debate, we can declare that we may deduce in both cases their corresponding contrary-to-fact conditionals. Thus, contrary-to-fact conditionals cannot be treated as an analysis of law-like universals. Sometimes it is supposed that the problem of dispositions is actually simpler than the problem of contrary-to-fact conditional and the problem of contrary-to-fact conditionals finds a way out through it. Dispositions are law like in essence. This view has been developed by Ryle[23], who holds that dispositional statements are "semi hypothetical". But to define a statement as law like is to produce a rational justification of such a statement. Once again, we face the problem of making a law-like and non-law-like statement. The truth of a dispositional statement ultimately depends upon the implicit use of the "laws" it involves. Thus, any successful analysis of dispositional concept necessitates a satisfactory analysis of law statements.

1. Laws and Inductive Generalization

The failure of the attempt to "Justify" law in terms of contrary-to-fact conditionals and dispositions appears to be the failure of giving the logical justification of "Laws of Nature". Conclusive verification of the laws of nature is not possible, so the demonstrative vindication of law like universal is an impossibility. Thus, our approach is to the problem of critical *acceptance* and not the problem of validation. The acceptance of law statements would be critical or rational. Some think that the rationality of law statements is constituted by inductive generalizations. A familiar and influential statement of this conception was given by John Stuart Mill. Briefly stated, Mill's view would be that law statements are empirical generalizations about the constitution of nature. The principle of the uniformity of nature, according to Mill, asserts that "there are such things in nature as parallel cases; that what happens once will, under a sufficient degree of similarity of circumstances, happen again"[24]. Mill undoubtedly believed that this statement has an empirical content, whether it does or not hinge on how one understands the expression "a sufficient degree of similarity of circumstances". When are circumstances sufficiently similar? A superficial resemblance between circumstances is obviously not enough. Two sets of circumstances may be judged to be alike even by trained and discriminating observers, yet an effect may follow upon one set but not upon another. It is patent that the expression "a sufficient degree of similarity of circumstances" is being so used that two sets of circumstances are said to be sufficiently similar only if they have similar consequences. On this assumption, Mill's formulation of the principle does not possess an empirical content. So it is difficult to maintain that law statements are empirical generalizations.

Mill's *supposed* law of the uniformity of nature on analysis turns out to be a *proposed* law of nature, for it cannot be shown to be empirical, *at least not to start with*. To get rid of this difficulty, the pragmatists suggest that whether a law is empirical or not is to be gathered from its consequences and not from its starting point or empirical basis. The pragmatist takes uniformity of nature as a postulate to organize experiences and act in the light of these experiences. The briefest and the most comprehensive formula for the method of pragmatism is, according to James, "the attitude of looking towards last things, fruits, consequences and facts"[25].

Peirce holds the view that the significance of a *thought* lies in the *action* to which it leads. Scientific laws are adopted because they work, i.e. because their consequences are satisfactory. A serious objection to the argument from the procedure of the sciences is derived from the ambiguity of the conception of "working". What sciences require of a working hypothesis is that it shall work theoretically, i.e. all its verifiable consequences shall be *true* and none *false*. We do not mean to state that it gives us emotional satisfaction; but that it does satisfy our aspirations. The working of law means its agreement with the observed facts. Thus, the kind of "working" which science accepts is different from the pragmatist notion of the word "working". When a scientist says that a hypothesis works, what he means is that the effects of believing it are good or useful and no *apriori* reason is shown as to why truth and utility should always go together. Consequently, it should be admitted that laws are not generalizations as the inductivists or pragmatists take them to be.

2. Logical Analysis of Law Statements: Hempel, Nagel and Black

Let us look into the logic of laws. Hempel, for instance, has shown[26] the particular difficulties in logically characterizing a statement as a law of nature. He is of opinion that law-like statements are statements of universal form and since any universal statement can be transformed into a conditional form, the paradigm expression for a law-like statement must be of the universal conditional in form. Hempel rightly thinks that the requirement of a universal conditional is not sufficient to characterize a statement as a law. For example, "Every apple in basket B at time T is red" is both true and of universal in form yet the statement does not qualify it as a law. One might suggest that the above statement is not a law, for it makes an assertion about a finite member of objects only. But are not Kepler's laws considered law like though they refer to finite set of planets only? So, it would be too much to deny the status of fundamental law-like statements to all statements which make an assertion about a finite class of objects only. It would rule out a statement such as "All robins' eggs are greenish blue" since the class of all robins' eggs—past, present and future—is finite. Again, there is a difference between this statement and the one above. For, in the former case, the meaning of the constitutive terms alone entails that it has a finite scope, whereas in the case of the latter, the empirical knowledge is relevant to establish the finiteness of robins' eggs. More specifically, the idea suggests itself of permitting a predicate in a fundamental law-like statement only if it is purely universal or purely qualitative, i.e. a statement or its meaning does not require reference to anyone particular object. But the stipulation just proposed suffers from the vagueness of the concept of purely qualitative predicates. This important point was also recognized by Nagel[27], who says that mere logical analysis or syntactical considerations do not fulfil the task of producing a definition for purely qualitative predicates. This aspect of the argument appears to be correct. On this point, Hempel's observation is such that since a natural language does not provide an explicit definition of meanings for its terms, provision for this would be with respect to a formalized language governed by well-determined system of logical rules. But the difficulty is precisely that of stating a rigorous criterion for the distinction between permissible and impermissible interpretations and it will present the same problem as a non-formalized language. To do this, what appears to be necessary is the help of a non-logical analysis of law-like universals. Due to some unavoidable difficulties involved in making rigid boundary between a law-like and non-law like conditionals, Nagel has come to the conclusion that any attempt to make such a distinction is bound to be arbitrary. That is why Nagel states that we are certainly free to designate any statement as a "law of Nature"[28]. But this line of reasoning is hardly convincing. Any or every statement cannot be treated as a law-like statement; the failure of logical analysis of law-statements need not entail the refutation of the arguments in favour of the acceptance of law-like statements.

As regards the problem of making a distinction between two kinds of generalizations, Black takes the help of logical considerations[29]. His line of argument is as follows: a connected (universal) conditional is logically equivalent with its corresponding contrapositive, while an accidental (universal) conditional is not to be treated as logically equivalent with its corresponding contrapositive. An accidental conditional and its corresponding contrapositive have different ranges of truth conditions of direct verification. But this is not case in a connected conditional. A connected as well as its corresponding contrapositive conditional are falsifiable, partially verifiable and openly unaffected by the same state of affairs; in consequence, the two are logically equivalent. It is true that traditional logicians accept the equivalence between a proposition of the form "All s is p" and the corresponding proposition of the form "All non-p is non-s". It is also true that they have not been challenged on this point, even though they have been challenged on many others. But there are reasons to suppose that the law of contraposition cannot be maintained on the traditional interpretation of universal proposition. It can be shown that the presence of existential import in the universal proposition has an unfavourable consequence for the law of contrapositon. If all hypotheses have an existential import, then the contrapositive hypothesis of the original, viz., "All non-black things are non-ravens" has an existential import. A necessary condition of the truth of the proposition is that there are non-black things. The expression "All non-black things are non-ravens" cannot be true in a world which does not contain non-black things. But it is too much to say that a necessary condition of the truth of the proposition "All ravens are black" is the existence of non-black things. On the other hand, the proposition "All ravens are black", according to the same principle of existential import, implies the existence of ravens; and will not be true if the world does not contain any raven. But it is again too much to say that the proposition "All non-black things are non-ravens" presupposes the existence of ravens: that the proposition cannot be true in a world which does not contain any raven. It then follows that there is a possibility which makes the one either false or pointless but makes the other neither false nor pointless. Thus, it is quite natural to claim that the two hypotheses under consideration are not equivalent when both are allowed to have an existential import.

The problem still remains. What would be the rational way of explaining the acceptance of law-like universals? What sort of character would the laws of nature possess? We would like to say that law-like universals are always "conjectured" or "formulated" hypothetico-deductively "on the basis of" previous experiences. But what exactly does it mean? Law-like universals are always conjectures—conjectures of a special type. Conjectures may be of either a deductive or of an inductive type. The logic of the formation of a law-like universal is always *deductive* and quite different from the psychological construction of the inductivists. In the inductive formulation of a law-like statement, we always start with certain *pure* empirical facts which serve as the *basis* of the construction. The very *basis* of this formulation stands for the validation of the formulated hypothesis. Hence arises a difficulty. What exactly is in the *basis* which is claimed for the justification of the construed law-like universal? How can we claim that the empirical *basis* serves as the necessary and sufficient condition for the validity of such a construction? On the *basis* of "pure experience", we cannot go *beyond* experience and as laws always transcend experience, the idea of inductive construction cannot make acceptance of laws sufficiently intelligible.

Let us now concentrate on the *deductive* formulation of the laws of nature. Here the word "deductively" is used to convey a special sense. On this construction, we do not deny the possibility of starting from "previous expériences" but later on, we transcend such a "basis". If a law is made up of previous experiences, its application must be restricted. But every law has a truth-claim and, as a matter of fact, it is influenced by the agent's previous experiences or background knowledge. So there is a difference between a deductive and inductive construction of the laws of nature. In our attempt to construct laws of nature deductively, we should point out that previous experience cannot be used as the rationality of the construed laws.

In the above context, we take the word "conjecture" seriously. Laws, being general description of structural properties of nature, are ontologically committed, i.e. realistic in import. The scientists, strictly speaking, describe nature in terms of laws. Laws are not of their own make or ascription. In the light of new empirical findings, a scientist is often obliged to modify or at least precisify the statement of laws. The findings which account for the modification or precisification of law statements are not themselves ascriptions. If the scientists could produce or ascribe the modifier, the precisifier, or the falsifier of the construed laws, without being constrained by the independent world of objects, could always defend the laws ascribed to the world by him, irrespective of the quality and quantity of relevant findings. Obviously, that is not the case. The history of science abounds with the instances of the changing carrier of laws—change brought about by the *real* and empirical findings. This clearly suggests that laws are to be *described* and not *ascribed*. Someone might insist, why should we call this formulation "deductive"? The answer seems to be that in our construction of law-like universals, we transcend the limits of our experience. This transcendence is possible by virtue of the dispositional character of the concepts involved in the very constitution of the laws. When we make a generalization "All fire burns", we already assume that the fire itself has the capacity to burn always. To this extent, there is "necessity" and this cannot be shown to be demonstratively. Demonstration presupposes (in some sense or other) of what is to be demonstrated. It is to be noted that the origin of this construction is always "empirical", whereas its validity is not so. The validity of a law-like statement (L) depends upon its consequences. L may possess an infinite number of consequences and if even one of them is in the form not-L, then L could not be regarded as "necessary". Therefore, there should be room for possible falsifiers in the realm of actual verifiers. But against this view, one might question what makes us believe in accepting the contrary existential statement that can test the truth of a law-statement? Or, to put it in other words, what makes such a perception of counter-evidence true? We may try to meet the charge in the following manner. The level at which we test the truth of a universal statement by ascertaining its relation of incompatibility or otherwise to the relevant existential statement is different from the level at which we test the truth of the latter itself by looking into its deducibility from "corresponding" universal statements and consistency with "collateral" existential statements. There is no such thing as "pure experience". Nor is there anything like "pure existence." Experience is always interpreted in the light of theories and expectations which are more or less transcendental in character. Statements which appear as purely existential or particulars are also universal, for the universal terms which essentially occur in them entail dispositions to behave in a law-like manner. Thus, laws of nature and other universals are construed symmetrically. The difference consists in the degree of universality and transcendence. Therefore, not only the higher level explanatory theories transcend experience but even the most ordinary existential statements also do the same. This is so because even ordinary existential statements contain universals and, therefore, cannot be reduced to experience as such. All universals are dispositional in varying degrees. The word "breakable" is clearly dispositional in a higher degree than is the word "broken". We may, therefore, distinguish between statements belonging to various levels of universality. The statements belonging to the higher level are axioms and that of the lower level can be deduced from the former, which in turn, can be falsified by pointing out their incompatibility with the well-established truths of every day life. But the so-called well-established statements are also, strictly speaking, hypothetical in character. In consequence, anybody, in principle, can question the truth of these relatively basic statements as well, but not at the level (of the truth-value determination) of higher order statements.

Finally, regarding the nature of the expression law-like universals, it can be claimed that they set limits to what is possible, i.e. that they have the character of prohibitions. One might say that laws are principles of impossibility with respect to certain conditions and they are contingent as compared with logical tautologies. They do not assert that something exists or is the case; they insist on the non-existence of certain things, or states of affairs. If we accept as true one singular statement which infringes the prohibition by asserting the existence of a thing ruled out by the law, then the law is refuted (at least temporarily).

We can never *know* definitely and conclusively whether a supposed law is a genuine law or an accidental universal. We can, however, prove by turning to certain initial conditions under which the supposed law turns out to be invalid, that it was not necessary. This means that the laws of nature are physically necessary with reference to certain conditions. It is part of the greatness and beauty of science that we can learn through our critical investigations that the world may quite different from what we take or imagine it to be unless, of course, our imagination itself is guided by the studied refutation of earlier theories. There does not seem to be any reason to think that this process will come to an end. Therefore, the task of reducing all the laws of nature to the "principles of necessitation" cannot be fulfilled. The validity of a natural law and a causal law is constituted by the richness of its content. The richness itself is defined in terms of the class of propositions derived or derivable from the law in question. The explanatory claim of law is not *necessarily* fulfilled.

3. Necessity and Contingency in Laws of Nature

An attempt to construct an adequate (explicit) characterization of natural laws encounters considerable difficulties. Broadly speaking, four types of theories have been put forward about the logical character of laws.

The first suggested by Locke and more recently developed and defended by W. Kneale, is that the laws of nature are principles of natural necessitation. The view finds strong opponents in Hume, Mill and Braithwaite.

A third view—one which Kneale attributes to Whitehead—maintains that laws of nature are conjectures about uniformities holding over limited regions of space for limited periods of time. Finally, Schlilck and F.P. Ramsey have argued that laws of nature do not have the character of prohibitions which are essentially true or false. None of these approaches appears to be adequate. Advocates of the "necessitation theory" have strongly contested the view propounded by Hume. Hume insists that it is senseless to suggest that a law of nature is a principle of necessitation, for it is unquestionably true that if the proposition "salt dissolves in water" is a principle of necessitation, then salts not dissolving in water (under any condition) would be absolutely impossible. What is impossible is inconceivable. Since we can quite easily conceive of salt remaining in water but not dissolving after the point of saturation, it does not follow that "salt dissolves in water" is necessary. Kneale accepts this as a formidable but not insuperable objection[30], for the ability to conceive the contradictory of a given law is no bar to its being or being considered a principle of necessitation. Kneale's argument is interesting but it hardly can be regarded as satisfactory. "Necessity" is not a blanket expression. Logico-mathematical necessity and natural (or scientific) necessity do not mean one and the same sort of necessity. "Necessity", as conceived by Kneale, is different from "necessity" as accepted in physical sciences. Mathematical necessity, being concerned with the numbers and well-defined relations is *formal* in character, while natural laws designed to connect and structurally describe natural events may be credited only with an empirical, i.e. a weaker sort of necessity. Kneale's argument attaches unjustified importance to the word "conceivable". "Inconceivability" in logic and mathematics is simply another name for leading to an obvious contradiction. Logically, "conceivable" is everything that does not lead to an obvious contradiction. When Kneale uses the word to indicate the contradiction of a theorem, he uses it in a different sense. Kneale seems to have attached exclusive importance to this latter sense, thereby tending to rule out the legitimate distinction between "logical" and "physical" necessity. Kneale uses it in a sense other than strictly logical or mathematical, i.e. the one mentioned above. This other sense may be a good sense, but it seems to smack of psychologism. To ignore the two senses of the word "necessity" is to indulge into confusion. An assumption may be wrongly defined as physically necessary if and only if its denial contradicts the laws of nature. Since these laws of nature are our conjectures, they are always open to tests. It is an another way of maintaining that an ability to "perceive" or "conceive" the contradictory instances of the laws of nature does falsify the natural laws and this falsifiability constitutes the truth or the necessity of the physical laws. Kneale might object to this view by stating that the inability to conceive the necessity of natural laws follows from our epistemic ignorance and it should not affect the objective validity of the natural laws. But we can meet this charge against us by saying that apart from epistemic apparatus, laws of nature cannot be made intelligible; hence epistemic considerations must enter into the real structure of the formulations of the laws of nature.

Advocates of the "contingent" view of natural laws have concentrated their attention on the facts of unrestricted universality. It is also the view adopted by Hume, who states that we often speak of natural laws as principles of necessary connection but he holds the view that this necessity is the projection of our expectation. To assert a law of nature is to assert a constant conjunction without restriction to the field of our actual experience. Since there cannot be facts of unrestricted universality or the sentences which intend to state such facts are meaningful, so this theory of Hume has been criticized. Facts are identical with the contingent truths of which we have spoken. There are thinkers who have assumed a connection between universality and necessity; no significant universal statement can be at once contingent and restricted. Necessity in Kantian epistemology has been confounded with universality. The unrestricted universal "All S is P" has necessity in the sense that it entails that if anything were S, it would also be P. It is a necessary proposition in the sense that it necessitates each S to be P. No one would be so foolish as to assert an unrestrictedly universal statement about the physical world on the ground of man's restricted experience. Therefore, we must have a non-factual source for claiming these statements to be true. For Kneale, it is not possible for us to conceive natural laws as facts of unrestricted or of restricted universality. If we consider a case of restricted universality, we invite troubles. It is true that laws of nature are normally expressible in the timeless present and concerned not only with the actual instances of some kind but with anything which might have satisfied a certain description. But an unfulfilled hypothetical proposition cannot be derived from a proposition which is concerned only with the *actual*. No doubt, there cannot be the experience of natural laws as facts of either restricted or of unrestricted universality. The point which to Kneal's mind is more fundamental is this: a logical distinction can be made between a law-like and a non-law like statement. The logical strength of a law-like universal lies in its power of sustaining an unfulfilled hypothetical proposition. But what is not clear to us in this: an unfulfilled conditional can be sustainable both by an accidental and by a non-accidental universal. It is possible only on the assumption that no *actuality* is intelligible without any reference to the notion of *possibility*. Therefore, if we consider that restricted as well as unrestricted universals are concerned only with the *actuals*, we should also admit that both these universals contain non-actuals (possibles) in their extensions; further if they contain non-actuals in their extension, then it follows that they may sustain two types of counter-factual conditionals.

The third view is that natural laws are restrictedly universal and we can speak of infinity only in connection with possibility and not in connection with actuality. This view has been defended, among others, by whitehead[31]. Whitehead believes that every empirical generalization must be limited *in use* and we can never have any warrant for making unrestricted generalizations about what happens in nature. But this view needs some elucidation. It is obvious that we express laws of nature in the present tense, but they are equally applicable to the future and the past, and there is nothing in the argument to show that the course of future events would come to a close or an end. This is so because the terms involved in stating the laws of nature are not mere substitutes for lists of proper names but unrestricted general descriptions. This view has been persuasively defended by Popper. Against this, Kneale argued in a paper contributed to Analysis in 1950 that Popper's theory would not do what he wanted of it, because, according to his understanding, it still allowed no room for drawing a tenable distinction between laws and merely accidental generalizations. In other words, Popper's position implies that there may be strictly universal statements which have an accidental character. In an appendix to Popper's logic of Scientific

Discovery of 1959, we find a clue to overcome that difficulty. Popper concedes that something more must be done to distinguish laws from accidental generalizations and offers a definition of "natural necessity". Such an account makes all laws naturally or physically necessary and excludes those generalizations which hold merely because of the *de facto* arrangements of the known things in the world. What holds for all *possible* worlds is obviously physically necessary and it means that every natural possibility must be realized somewhere at some time or at least in *principle* be realizable. This view seems to be unexceptionable.

The fourth view is that laws of nature are prescriptions or maxims of conduct. This doctrine has been developed by a number of positivists. Schlick, for instance, states that natural laws are rules of behaviour for anticipating certain events. Since laws of nature have unrestricted universality, they look like statements and cannot be verified in experience. Since verification in experience constitutes the mark of a significant statement, Schlick interprets the laws of nature as prescriptions. But laws of nature cannot be treated as prescriptions for several reasons. In fact, laws do describe and are expressive of the structural properties of the world; it is not merely an epistemological or logical construct. Laws are admittedly fallible, and fallibility cannot be significantly predicated of what is instrumental or prescriptive in character. It is also true that natural laws may be construed as maxims of conduct and answering some of our psychological needs of character, that but that does not mean they are subjective in origin. In that case, the universality of natural laws remains unexplained. This peculiarity can be overcome if we consider natural laws as expressive of the real structural properties of the world. As to the internal structures of the laws of nature, we accept, the fact that people may understandably differ because of the diverse conditions— subjective and objective—under which the structural properties of the world are apprehended by us. It is only fair enough on our part to admit that man's capacity to apprehend nature has a situational limit and this limit is set by his intellectual and sociological background. It follows then, that if we conjecture P as a natural law, we conjecture that it expresses a structural property of our world by declaring the impossibility of certain events and the principle would have to be tested by trying to prove that these events are possible.

In passing, it is interesting to note that the view suggesting that laws of nature are logically necessary faces grave objections, Firstly, the formal denials of the laws of positive science are not self-contradictory at least not demonstratively or manifestly. So these cannot be described as logically necessary. Secondly, if laws of nature are logically necessary, then the procedure appropriate to a supposed law must be nearer to that of constructing a demonstrative proof in the manner of mathematics and not that of experimentation. The assumption that laws of nature must be logically necessary does not follow from the fact that it is essential for explanation and prediction. Hence, the assumption requires such a characteristic that plays no identifiable part in the actual use of the law. A law of nature is necessary in its turn because it is logically derivable from, or explicable by, a law of higher order of universality or of greater depth. A true scientific hypothesis is a law of nature only if it has an explanatory function with regard to lower-order hypothesis. This view, in spite of its diverse interpretations, has been maintained, among others, by Braithwaite, who believes that the conditions of an established hypothesis being law like will be that in an established scientific deductive system either it occurs as a higher-level hypothesis containing theoretical concepts or it occurs as a deduction from a higher level hypothesis, in an established scientific system[32]. The proposition in a deductive system may be considered as being arranged in order of levels. To the extent a scientific hypothesis provides an explanation, it may be endowed with the honourable status of natural law. Every "good" scientific theory or law is one which *forbids* the happening of certain events in a certain space-time region; the more a theory forbids the better it is. A natural law which is not refutable by any conceivable event is non-scientific but not necessarily useless. Every genuine test of a natural law is an attempt to falsify it or to refute it. Testability is falsifiability but there are degrees of testability; some are more testable than others. An individual might object to this view by arguing that the falsification of a natural law is just as impossible as its verification. This object conflates two different levels of analysis. At one level, there is a logical asymmetry. One singular statement can formally falsify natural laws, but these cannot be formally verified by any number of singular statements. The attempt to minimize the asymmetry can only lead to confusions. At another level, we may hesitate to accept any statement—even the simplest observation statement. We may also point out that every singular statement involves interpretation in the light of theories and is, therefore, certain. There cannot be anything like a completely safe observation free of the dangers of misinterpretation. The "empirical basis" largely consists of a mixture of theories of lower degree of universality. But the investigator can test a law by questioning at another level whatever he accepts as its "basis". The belief that science proceeds from observation to laws is still so widely and so firmly held that any denial of it is often met with incredibility. The belief that we can start with *pure* observation only without anything in the nature of a theory is pre-reflective and indefensible; observation is selective, it needs a chosen object, a definite task, an interest, a point of view, a problem. Popper has argued this view[33] most forcefully and effectively. One may still raise the question: "what causes first, the observation or the hypothesis?" It reminds us of another question, "what comes first, the hen or the egg?" The reply to the latter is "an earlier kind of egg"; to the former, "an earlier kind of hypothesis". Whatever hypothesis we choose is preceded by observations—the observations which it is designed to explain. But these observations, in turn, presuppose a frame of reference, a frame of expectations. If they created a need for explanation and thus gave rise to the invention of a hypothesis, it is because they could not be explained within the old framework of expectations. Since the fate of a law—its acceptance or rejection—is decided by observations and experiment, the principle of empiricism is fully preserved. As long as a law stands up to the severest tests we can design, it is accepted; if it does not, it is rejected; but it is never inferred from the empirical evidence. Hume, for instance, showed that it is not possible to infer a law from observational statements but this does not affect the possibility of refuting a law by the same. The method of trial-and-error is one of eliminating false theories by observational statements and the "justification" for this is the purely logical relationship of deducibility which allows us to assert the falsifiability of universal statements if we accept the truth of related singular ones. Someone might ask: why is it reasonable to prefer a non-falsified statement to falsified ones? The correct answer is: we search for truth (even though we can never be sure we have found it) and because non-falsified laws may still be true. Besides, we do not prefer any non-falsifiable theory or laws—only one which is well tested, and of which we think or hope that it will stand up to further tests. To say that the future will be like the past in the sense that the laws of nature will not change is unacceptable. It is reasonable to believe that the future will be very different from the past in many vitally important respects, and it is also perfectly reasonable to act on the assumption that it will, in many respects, be like the past, and that tested laws will continue to hold since we can have no better assumption to act upon. It is equally right to think that some of the laws upon which we rely may easily prove to be so unreliable that such a course of action will lead at times into serious trouble and we shall not continue to call it a "Law of nature". We search for natural laws and our belief in any natural law cannot have a safer basis than our successful attempts to refute it. We are interested in a hypothesis with a high degree of corroboration.

It would be a mistake to conclude from the above statements that we are interested in highly *probable* hypotheses. The probability of a statement is inverse to the content or the explanatory power of the statement. Accordingly, every interesting and powerful statement must have a low probability and, vice versa, a statement with a high probability will be scientifically uninteresting and have no explanatory power. Although we seek hypotheses with a high degree of corroboration, we do not seek highly probable hypotheses, i.e. powerful and improbable hypotheses. It is another way of saying that all laws are essentially tentative, conjectural or hypothetical. Before a law has been refuted, we never know in what way it may have to be modified. In consequence, a statement is a natural law if it is general in some respect, i.e. it does not refer to unique objects, has been empirically corroborated in some domain in a satisfactory way (for the time being) and belongs to some theory (i.e. incorporation in some system or theory) however rudimentary it might be. But it should be recorded immediately that not all the laws recognized in the sciences are of one type and that a scientific explanation is often regarded as satisfactory even though the laws cited in the premises are not "causal" in any usual sense. Before we proceed further, it is necessary to discuss the nature of causal laws.

4. Causal Laws

It is not easy to clearly define the notion of natural law and, therefore, it is very difficult to pick "causal laws" out from the class of natural laws. Many scientific laws, in fact, fail to meet some further condition such as that of being "causal laws". Russell defines causal law "as a general principle in virtue of which, given sufficient data about certain regions of space-time, it is possible to infer something about certain other regions of space-time"[34]. Russell also thinks that the inference may be only probable, but if the principle in question is good enough to be called "causal law", the probability should be considered more than a half. It is obviously a very wide definition. Under this definition, many common sense generalization such as "Fire burns", "Birds fly" are to be regarded as causal. Granted that these generalizations are not without exceptions; even then we make a distinction between scientific laws and statements expressing mere regularity. Scientific laws are formulated in such a way that they seem to be strictly universal although possible falsifying conditions may easily be imagined. Our knowledge about the physical world, as Russell understands, depends upon the main assumption that there are causal laws. Causality, as we understand it in the scientific method, is intended to connect and explain some events in abstraction from the rest. Causal laws connect the events perceived and unperceived. These laws present a spatio—temporal continuity involving no direct relation between events at a finite distance from each other. Instead of stating that one event A is followed by another event B, scientific laws state the functional relation between certain events at certain times and other events at earlier or later times or even at the same time. The view that within science causal laws state nothing but a functional dependency of a certain sort has also been defended, among others, by Carnap. He is of opinion[35] that of the two four-dimensional areas which are in temporal proximity, i.e. which follow one another, and between which the dependency obtains, we call the earlier one the *cause* of the latter, while this latter area is called the *effect* of the earlier. As to the inadequacy of the Russell-Carnapian formulation of the causal law, it can be said that a causal law expresses something more than the category of mere relation; it expresses a category of *genetic* connection, i.e. a way of *producing* things out of other things. A law of correlation is not a causal law; it can never say that a given entity is produced by another entity. Rather, the two are regularly associated. Furthermore, there are numerical laws which state a degree of interdependence between magnitudes so that variation in one of these is accompanied with variations in the others for which causal explanation is not possible. In the case of numerical laws, the relation of dependence between variables is symmetrical so that a state of the system at a given time is completely determined by either a later or an earlier one. But causal laws express an asymmetrical relation in the sense that heat causes expansion in the object while expansion does not cause heat in the object. Assuming laws of nature—including the causal ones—are functional in character, as Carnap believes, do we need to postulate any structural property exhibited by causal laws? No, if the *Carnapian* later formulation is correct. Carnap finds that a function of a law is to state a great deal about the world. Being universal in scope, its confirmation becomes impossible. Stronger verification theory given by the positivists led us to the conclusion that laws are meaningless. Popper points out that Catnap's theory of confirmation willy-nilly comes to the conclusion that laws are meaningless. Carnap has said that the acceptability of an inductive generalization depends upon its qualified-instance confirmation of the form that the next case of raven to be observed will be black. Confirmation may be a liberalized version of verification; nevertheless it ends in confessing that laws may be meaningful but unnecessary. This is a hopeless state of affairs. It means that the scope of universal is infinite, but the verifiers are so limited the verification value becomes zero. To say this is to argue that laws, strictly speaking, are not necessary for prediction. A singular predictive inference is the most important kind of inference. This unfailingly reminds one of Mill's arguments in support of inference from particular to particular. Since in scientific investigation, we always depend upon laws, including causal one, it is not possible to endorse the view that they are unnecessary. In this connection, it would be instructive to follow the line of another inductivist, Reichenbach. By a causal law Reichenbach[36] means a relation of the form "if-then with the addition that the same relation holds at all times". To say that the electric current causes a deflection of the magnetic needle means that there is *always* a deflection of the magnetic needle. The addition *always* distinguishes the causal law from a chance coincidence. An exceptionless repetition constitutes the meaning of a causal relation but it cannot exhaust the entire meaning content of a causal relation. It is not mistaken to hold that there may be a historical accident on the cosmic scale. So, in order to make a distinction between causal laws and chance coincidences we should take the help of the concept of (physical) necessity. Reichenbach tries to defend the causal principle in the following manner:

Since we have observed that the same function governs a finite number of observations, we conclude that it governs *all* observations[37].

This conclusion is not based upon the presupposition that causality holds in certain cases, i.e. we observe that certain laws hold in *particular* instances, and we infer that the laws will hold in *all* instances. If it is true that causality holds in other cases, it is only on the basis of the relevant governing function that this probability can be measured. The characterization of the causal laws of nature as strict laws of nature is based on certain assumptions. An effect can be predicted with certainty only when all the causal factors are known. To know all the causal factors is impossible and in order to predict future events, we can select only a limited number of relevant factors neglecting the factors of lesser importance. In the light of this assumption, Reichenbach proceeds to formulate a rigorous definition of the inductive principle of causality, guided as he claims, by the procedure of the physicists. He begins by formulating a function which serves as a hypothesis which will be true or false if the test supplies quantitative confirmation. A function expresses a law only when it describes an objective state and is independent of the accidental observational data. A function serves as a law of nature only because it is supposed that it will remain the same when the sequence is extended to any number of further measurements. In fact, laws of nature—including the causal ones—may satisfy certain descriptive functions, but they are not expressing structural or real properties of the world. On this interpretation, a causal law asserts an invariable statistical relation between properties or events. These laws assert that the prediction of a *class* of one kind is accompanied by the occurrence of a *class* of different kinds. These laws are not incompatible with the causal account of the facts, although they are not manifestly causal. On the other hand, there are also statistical laws in physics for which at present no causal explanations are known. Statistical interpretation of causal laws, as formulated by Reichenbach, cannot account for the element of productivity between the earlier and later states. This formulation should not be accepted like any other empiricist formulation of the laws of nature. Granting that laws of nature are statistical in character, and if Reichebach's thesis is correct, there is no need to postulate the structural causal properties of nature. But this defens simultaneously raises an undesirable consequence. It is not the statistical character that constitutes the causal structures of the world; rather there are good reasons to suppose that the real structure of nature may be statistically expressed for some specific purposes.

Causal law, as characterized by Nagel[38], seems to accord with our intuitive idea of a causal situation connecting certain events. He offers certain conditions which every causal law must satisfy and they are as follows:

(1) The relation between the antecedent and the consequent of a universal causal conditional is an invariable or uniform one, i.e. whenever the alleged cause occurs, so does the alleged effect. It indicates that the cause constitutes both a necessary and a sufficient condition for the occurrence of the effect.

(2) The antecedent and the consequent of a universal causal conditional are spatially contiguous, i.e. the cause and the effect occur approximately in the same spatial region.

(3) The antecedent and the consequent of a universal causal conditional are temporarily continuous, i.e. the event said to be the cause precedes the effect and is also "continuous" with the latter.

(4) The antecedent and the consequent of a universal causal conditional are related asymmetrically.

I have not the slightest desire to deny the above conditions stated by Nagel to indicate which of the universal conditionals may be regarded as causal laws. But certain clarifications are called for. The invariability of the relation between a cause and its effect cannot be ascertained absolutely. Otherwise a single variation of the law would not render the law modified. And, at the same time, it is interesting to note that the notion of productivity is involved in the notion of invariability in a causal domain. Here, one may suggest that productivity is not to be treated as the essence of causality. This fact can be proved theoretically; otherwise it would not be possible to distinguish a causal proposition from a non-causal one. Being conscious of the characters assigned to the causal law, we may now construct its form in the following way: "If cause happens then (and only then) effect is *always* produced by it". To assign the above characters to the causal law is to distinguish it from those laws *that* are not truly causal. Developmental laws, for instance, which can be formulated in this way: "If X has the property P at one time T, then X has the property Q at later time T", may supply a necessary condition for the occurrence of the effect, but they do not supply the sufficient condition for the occurrence of the effect. Since these laws cannot account for the uniqueness of relation between events, they cannot be characterized as causal laws.

Before I conclude, I would like to point out one other thing. If the line of argument developed is correct, then causal laws are to be regarded as part and parcel of the world. Explanation is either an explanation of a problem or a problematic aspect of an event. Causal laws explain only the typical productive aspects of the events in question. But all laws of nature are not causal.

CHAPTER III

Action and Explanation

B roadly speaking, there are two types of disciplines—nomothetic and ideographic. Nomothetic sciences seek to establish abstract general laws for indefinitely repeatable events and processes, while the ideographic sciences aim to understand those phenomena which are unique in character. It is also claimed that the social sciences, as distinguished from the natural ones, are mainly concerned with the description of particular events or actions, and the logical structure of the concepts and explanations required in this type of sciences is fundamentally different from that of the concepts used and explanations offered by the natural sciences. My attempt in the present chapter will be to determine the exact nature of the explanation of human actions. The story of a man's life is the story of man's actions and the things that happen to him. What distinguishes a human action from a natural movement? This debate is not likely to prove interesting unless we find answers to some other relevant questions, such as: what precisely is an action? Are human actions determinable or not? I shall further try to investigate why causal explanation of human actions, at its best, is found to be unsatisfactory. This will finally lead to the point that human actions are to be explained in terms of "reason".

1. Actions and Physical Movements

To act is to bring about something. Action is the opening up of man to other men and the world. It is intelligible only as the expression and fulfilment or frustration of the actor's inner purpose. When, for example, I strike a matchstick against a matchbox, the striking is a movement no doubt, but it is definitely something more than mere movement—it is an action performed by me. If, on the other hand, a man strikes me and I fall, my falling is a movement, which happens to me; it is capable of being explained in purely mechanical terms where purpose plays no role. If an action is always someone's action, if an action has a necessary reference to the agent's choice or decision (which may designate as its "inner side"), then it is something for which the agent must be prepared to accept the responsibility. The part played by purpose or intention in explaining an action has been emphasized, among others, by Malcolm Knox[39]. Knox rightly thinks that if a man's intention is a genuine one, then there would be no gap in the continuity between the crystallization of intention—which is the "inner side" of an action—and the doing, which is its "outer side". Human actions express an individual's response to his environment. No definition of an action can be complete unless action is recognized as *response* and *creativity*. Human actions absolutely subject to the laws of nature cannot be creative, but viewed from the aspect of mind, it cannot be wholly devoid of creativity.

We will now attempt to distinguish "doing" from "happening". Happening can be predicted but it makes little sense to say that happening can be intended. Whatever happens, happens according to the laws of nature, whether we intend them or not. But "doing" is not to be regarded as such an automatic action or just a re-action. The notion of agency belongs to it essentially. The problem now arises: how can we rationally explain an action? Some thinkers believe that the explanation of an action aims at showing that the action in question was not a "matter of chance", but was to be expected in view of certain antecedent or simultaneous conditions. This expectation is not a privacy or divination, but rational scientific explanation on the basis of general laws. Objectivity of history or the study of actions consists, partly at least, in the predictability of human actions. If historical study is to be treated with respect and not merely as an expression of personal idiosyncrasies, it has to be objective. Its objectivity implies its universal character, its impartiality, impersonality, communicability and repeatability. If human actions possess these qualities, they must be predictable just as physical events and their explanations also would be of the some type, i.e. causal.

Explanation of a phenomenon, whether physical or human, would consist in its subsumability under appropriate general laws. The belief that the structure of the explanation of human actions is identical with that of causal explanation used in natural sciences is based on the assumption that both human and natural laws are prescriptions. While the former regulate and control the behaviour of human beings, the latter regulate and control the behaviour of nature. But it is also true that historical laws or human laws are more complex and variable than the natural ones. This is mainly due to freedom and thought of human agents who, under given conditions, create or weave the patterns of history. The elements of freedom and thought introduce another dimension in human affairs and that is creative in character. In other words, human laws are, in most cases, the rules of conduct. They prescribe the things one ought to or ought not to do. Natural laws do not prescribe the course of happenings. Because of this fundamental difference, the laws that causally explain the occurrence of natural events cannot by any manipulation exhaustively explain human actions. Natural laws explain natural events in the sense that they constitute the "necessary" as well as "sufficient" conditions for the happening of an event. But such laws are sometimes "insufficient" for the purpose of the explanation of human action. The uniqueness of human action poses a problem which cannot be satisfactorily tackled within the relatively rigid framework of natural explanation. Hence the question arises: are human actions determinable? Can we say that human actions necessarily proceed from conscious motives, desires or intentions?

2. Actions and its Causal Determinations

Historically speaking, this debate can be traced to the times of Aristotle, Spinoza, etc. One view which has recently gained ground (although one can trace its beginning even during Aristotle) is that in action, the cause of the movement is simply the agent himself. An agent has the power to affect the world producing actions. Aristotle felt[40] it necessary to distinguish voluntary actions from involuntary actions. Voluntary actions spring from within and are partly controlled by the actor or agent and involuntary actions originate from without and there is little or nothing which the actor can contribute to this sort of action. For Aristotle, choice involves a rational principle or thought and we make choice about the means of a voluntary action, action done by putting in our own effort. We assume the end and deliberate how and by what means it is to be attained. Thus, the choice is a "deliberate desire of things in our own power" or, as Aristotle puts it, "it is either desireful reason or reason-ful desire". Deliberation is about the things to be done by the agent himself but actions are for the sake of things other than themselves. It is interesting in this connection to note that Aristotle is offering a teleological explanation of human action in so far as he believes that actions aim at something other than itself and from its tendency to produce this end, it deserves its value. Value of an action lies in its ability to bring the agent nearer to the good which constitutes the end of men. Each action has an ultimate end which is valuable in itself and Aristotle firmly believed that the ultimate end of actions must be one. If all actions are looked upon as performances for the fulfilment of "one end" then action are, in a sense, *necessary*. Yet, in Aristotle's scheme, there is an apparent contingency in the realm of human actions. Choice or "rational desire", being the efficient cause of human actions, cannot causally determine its consequence. But this *indetermination* has little importance in Aristotle's scheme. In assessing this theory, we can state that a cause is an event which is correlated with its subsequent event by a law so that we can appeal to the prior event to explain the subsequent one. But we have no grounds for *prediction* of any particular action if all we know is only that some particular action was produced by the agent. In sum, it would appear that we no longer have the possibility of prediction, or causal laws, and hence no causal theory at all. But it is not clear to us whether or not Aristotle would believe that agent causation is incompatible with event-causation.

Spinoza's[41] rigid determinism compels him to declare that human actions are determined events. Human beings are finite modes within the single deductive system which Spinoza calls "God" or "Nature". The actual servitude and happiness of man and his ideally possible freedom and happiness are both to be impartially deduced as necessary consequence of his status as a finite mode in nature. Every finite mode endeavours to preserve itself and increase its power of self preservation. But this self-maintenance is not the outcome of choice or decision. It occurs naturally and necessarily to all things in nature. That human beings are capable of making a free choice is a superstition. And if it is possible to show that every human action is to be deducible from a law of nature, then there is at least one sense in which we must say that the agent could not in this case have acted otherwise, i.e. no alternative action was possible. But, as human beings are essentially free and the attempt to characterize free as the result of our ignorance is only an inexact understanding, Spinoza is certainly right in declaring that a "cause" is that which explains the existence of the effect and "explanation" exhibits a necessary connection. But our objection to this view is that will, choice or desire can never be treated as *necessary* causes of human actions; these can influence human actions.

Hobbes offers[42] a purely deterministic explanation of human action—of course, from a different point of view. He defines philosophy or scientific knowledge as knowledge of effects or appearances which we acquire by true ratiocination; from the knowledge of their causes or generation. Hobbes identifies cause with antecedent motion. The traditional Aristotelian doctrine was that everything moves towards the natural end or final goal. Hobbes thinks that in the world of bodies, final cause has no part to play. A world of bodies composed of particles is moved by other bodies and other particles. Hobbes' bridging concept was "endeavour"[43] which enabled him to describe human behaviour in terms of his general theory of motion. There is a close continuity between what we do and what we ought to do, i.e. between the actual and the ethical. To say this is to suggest that all human actions are caused or determined, being prompted by some endeavour of motion, fear, revenge, love, etc. A man is free to perform an action according to his will without any external constraint. But it makes no sense to say that man's will is free, for will or desire or inclination proceeds from some causes. So, actions done on choice are explicable in terms of antecedent causes as we explain the motion of anything else in the universe. But can we not draw a distinction between "endeavour of motion" and "endeavor of mover"? Perhaps we can. Further, since there is no room for personal agency and there is nothing in this account that is "my doing"—man is a creature and not creator of his conditions, physiological and physical. If desires, volitions are the causal factors, and these are subject to causal explanation in terms of antecedent psychological factors, then what happens is none of man's own doing. Hence, it is those causal factors that are happening in us rather than things that we do. All these things are somehow brought about by (means of) prior happenings of like sort. Consequently, all our thoughts degenerate into purely natural phenomena wholly exempt in principle from rational appraisal, which is really unsatisfactory.

It is of some interest here to recall the views of Collingwood who believes in the causal explanation of human action. Collingwood argues[44] that it is possible to explain human actions causally if we take "cause" in the historical sense of the term. Cause and effect in history refer to these type of cases in which both are human activities. What is caused is the free and deliberate act of a conscious, responsible agent; "causing," means, "making", "inducing", "forcing", "persuading", etc. For Collingwood, an action would be deliberate only if it is caused, though, of course, the cause may come into operation through the act of a second conscious and responsible agent. It means that the second person may put the first in a certain situation in such a manner that the first now believes himself to be in a certain situation and he persuades the first to form a certain intention. If A causes B to do an act C, C is B's own act, it is not A's act and Collingwood is of opinion that B is a free agent in doing C, and responsible for it as well. There is no contradiction in saying that the act C was caused by A and B was responsible for it. In that case, we cannot say that A is not responsible for the doing of C; A is responsible for its own act of pointing out certain things to B, by the help of which he persuades B to commit the act C. Again, it is perfectly possible for a man to act on his own responsibility when his knowledge about the situation is not dependent on the suggestion of others; in that case a man can be said to cause his own action as well as to do it. To say this is to hold that the choosing agent is the free "cause" of his acts in the sense that the knowledge of his situation influences his course of action in that particular situation. But this influence is fundamentally different from the constraint which natural laws impose upon the happenings of natural events. Collingwood's approach is justified in the sense that explanation as causal in the case of human actions is different from the causal explanation as applied to natural events. Then, would it not be reasonable to designate the explanation of human action as something different from the explanation used in the case of natural happenings? An agent, being a *free person*, can never come under causal relation (cause in the sense of a necessary and sufficient condition). Thus, causal relation fails here. If Collingwood's line of argument would express such a consequence, there can be no objection against him.

3. Kant on Human Actions

It is to Kant we owe the most clear-cut distinction between (moral or free) reason of action and cause of (bodily) motion (or, in an inexact sense, action). Kant believes[45] that human actions are performed in accordance with a maxim or universal principle or law and this distinguishes them from animal behaviour. Such maxims or principles normally arise from the cooperation of reason and inclination. There are subjective as well as objective principles. Subjective principles are those on which the individual agent chooses to act. Objective principles are those on which any rational being would act if reason has full control over his inclinations. Kant uses the ethical term "maxim" to designate a subjective principle of action. A maxim is the principle of determining the ground of man's actions which is distinct from an objective principle on the one hand and from a motive on the other. Unlike an objective principle, it holds good only for the person acting in accordance with it, unlike a motive, it can be generalized as being the ground of man's particular activities. Kant distinguishes between two types of maxims—a posteriori or material maxims and a priori or formal maxims. A posteriori maxims are the maxims based on empirical or sensuous inclinations. A priori maxims are not based on empirical or sensuous inclinations. A man who shows his good will, in acting for the sake of duty and nothing else, is acting on a formal maxim of duty and, as such, his action is a moral action. This moral law of duty may be formulated thus: "I shall do my duty whatever my duty may be". This is a universal law followed for its own sake by the rational agent if reasons have had full control over inclinations. Thus, the moral law or the law of freedom and the natural law posses a common characteristic, namely universality. But, while moral law under human conditions appears to us as command or imperative, there is nothing like this in natural law. There are hypothetical as well as categorical imperatives. When the objective principle of the practical reason of an action is conditioned by an end, the imperative is hypothetical. When the objective principle of practical reason is not conditioned by an end, and the purpose of an act is enjoyed for its own sake as a good in itself, the imperative is categorical. Every rational agent, according to Kant, ought to will thus.

It seems evident that when Kant treats will to be a power to act in accordance with the rational man's conception of laws, he treats will as a power to produce effect. Only this will is a self-caused cause, not determined by external constraints. In nature, the causal action of an efficient cause is itself caused by something else and hence its action is not spontaneous. The laws of morality are self-imposed; hence the moral agent, in a sense, is free. He is certainly not free in the sense that he possesses a "law less" free will. Will is "free cause" because its spontaneous actions take place in accordance with self-imposed law. Every moral action is, thus, a law-governed action. A free will is such that must be conceived as capable of acting as maxims which can, at the same time, be willed as universal laws and this is the principle of moral action. It follows, therefore, that a free will and a will working under moral laws is one and the same thing. But it does not seem clear as to how a particular activity can possibly attain its moral character in conformity with the universal timeless moral law. If Kant is to think of a man as acting freely in accordance with timeless moral laws, he has also to think of the world as the world of things as they are in themselves and not as they appear to our senses. Here, we are not interested in the explanation of actions which is not a temporal event in terms of non-temporal moral principle. The will which has been characterized by Kant as a "free cause" is not will in our ordinary sense of the term. It is a space-time invariant will; it cannot produce a temporal action. But we fail to understand what sort of thing a timeless action is. Thus, Kant's conception of will causality cannot help us to make intelligible the occurrences of our everyday actions which are temporal events.

Kant's interpretation of human actions has been criticized, among others, by Stuart Hampshire. Hampshire's main aim is to show that human action is essentially intentional and its intentionality cannot be ascertained by a rule or by a criterion; we are immediately aware of its intentional character. We agree with Hampshire to a large extent. An action is intentional if it is backed by a particular type of ability, viz., intentional ability. This ability is never a matter of perception; it is a matter of immediate apprehension. That I am an intentional agent is known immediately. Thus, the intentional character of human action is self-evident and not language-evident. Verbalization or verbalizability, linguistic reproduction or linguistic reproducibility is not a necessary condition for the proof of the identity of an intentional action. Kant might agree that he is interested only in *ideal* action and not in what we call space-time bound *actual* action. It is again throwing back to the distinction between *bodily* act and *mental act*—in a way to the body-mind dualism. In effect, it leads to an undesirable consequence.

Human actions are never determined. Thought cannot dictate action. Kant's theory of rule-governed nature of actions makes undertaking of a moral enquiry an idle job. Man's action can never be explained by a universal moral law; rather a man's ability is always limited by his body, situation, space, time, etc. This means that alternative explanations of human action are always possible. As all the parameters of actions are unavailable to man, he must be moral always within some limitations. To say this is to hold the view that a man enjoys a situational freedom and that his actions are determined. If every one of our actions are determined by antecedent causes, it follows that we could not have acted in any way other than the manner in which we actually did. As those actions that we must perform are unavoidable, it is futile to exhort us with an *ought* when we are forced to comply with a *must*. Moral pursuit would be a barren pursuit unless our action proves to be an exception to the principle that every event is determined by antecedent causes. In human discourse, we are concerned not with the discovery of the rules for action, but with the description of consciousness which is intentional, which is in the consciousness of the situation where he is an ethical agent. The content of a human action is a chosen content but its choice is being "determined" by our own value consciousness. Consequently, human actions cannot be considered as free (rule governed) as Kant declares.

4. Action and its Non-Causal Determinations

It is interesting in this connection to follow the arguments of those philosophers who are unwilling to accept the demand that human actions are causally determined. Notable among they are: Melden, Nowell-Smith, Ryle, and Hampshire. In connection with the problem of the relation between a motive and action, Melden argues[46] that the presence of a motive cannot be treated either as a necessary or a sufficient condition for an action to occur. Melden restricts the use of the term to the case of intentions. The logical connection between a motive and its action is possible if the motive was some event—either concurrent or antecedent to the action. This is impossible if the "motive action" is a causal sequence. Given the statement of the motive, an action can be explained in twofold ways: (1) by placing the action in its appropriate context, a motive provides with a better understanding of the action; and (2) a motive of an action reveals something about the person himself. It is true that this is completely different from the causal explanation of an action, since a person may refrain from acting though he has a specific motive in mind for acting in a particular way. We cannot call the motive a sufficient condition of the action. Since a person may act without being prompted by a motive, it cannot be called its necessary condition either. Thus, a motive or any other event cannot be related causally to its action. Melden is surely right in his approach to the problem in saying that motives cannot refer to some other event which can causally explain how the action came to be.

Nowell-Smith,[47] for example, agrees with us to a large extent. He is also in favour of the view that we cannot predict "What we shall do" but we can decide "What we shall do". There cannot be any necessary connection between a man's deciding and acting because what the mind decides today may change tomorrow. A change of mind may be sudden but inexplicable. If a man has decided to do something and does not do it, then either the man changed his mind or was prevented from doing. This argument proves the failure of the mental cause theory about the explanation of human action. Ryle[48] also claims that an explanation in terms of a motive is different from an explanation in terms of its cause. Explanations for motives are explanations in terms of dispositions, tendencies, and abilities to act in a certain manner. A motive is not an event or force inside us which functions as an antecedent cause, but what is striking is this: motive explanations should not be confused with the mere dispositional explanation. Dispositions only tell us the possibility of occurrence of events, they do not tell us of the occurrence as such. Thus, the Rylean form of the dispositional analysis cannot sufficiently recognize the occurrent character of human action.

On the above question, Hampshire's opinion is noteworthy. He thinks[49] that the notion of doing any thing is unintelligible without the notion of intentionality. Prediction is not possible in the realm of action and intention has no relevance to the happenings of nature. An intentional actor intending its object goes out of itself and attempts to achieve its end completely. This view of internal and persistent continuity between the self-positing action and its other-intending aspect is clearly opposed to the atomic view of psychological action according to which an action is a sort of reaction to a stimulus. Atomists believe that the connection between a self-positing action and its other-intending character is always the result of past cumulative experience of a performed habit. This account is an indirect attempt to minimize the importance of freedom in action. That is quite unsatisfactory. Though human actions cannot be predicted, there is a kind of certainty about human actions. This certainly is not inductive certainty, based on empirical evidence. It is based on reason and may be called decision. That a person's announcement of his intention to do some action in the future is not a case of prediction is evident from the fact that if the person does not act as he says, this expresses him not to the criticism that what he said was false, but to the fact that he has changed his mind. What I shall do in the intermediate period between what I am doing immediately and what I shall be doing immediately cannot be predicted as a natural phenomena. This approach to human action is bound to remind us of the non-causal model of explanation.

It has rightly been pointed out that human actions are not entirely determined. Moral life suffers from endeavours. It is a mode of living guided by interests and intelligence of man in the right direction. For this reason, the power to decide otherwise is always possible. Consequently, the best model of explaining action would be intentional, or teleological. Actions are said to be teleological, if and only if, they are directed to the realization of a purpose or end. Further, the relation between a goal intended and an action done is non-causal. Intentions, motives or desires can influence an action but do not cause or determine them. Thus, "explanations of actions" would be "explanations in terms of reason". We may call such explanations *rationalizations*, and say that the reason rationalizes the action. At this stage, can we say that rationalization is a species of causal explanation? This question requires some clarifications.

5. Reasons and Actions

An explanation which consists of a description in terms of end, result or goal aimed at is often called a teleological explanation. In favour of the teleological thesis, it can be pointed out that here we do have a kind of explanation, which is often referred to as one of the forms of rationalization. Controversy arises when philosophers go on to claim that we have here a kind of explanation irreducibly different from and incompatible with ordinary causal explanation. It is this claim that we must examine. Even if we follow—just for the sake of argument—that a future event can causally affect a present event, we can easily dispose of the doctrine so far as the explanation of an action is concerned. It cannot be the case that every action is produced by the future goal state towards which it aims for the simple reason that in many cases, at least, the future goal state, is never achieved. Since the appropriateness of reason-explanations of actions does not force us to accept a special, unique and irreducible kind of explanation, we simply have here a special *kind* of explanation, viz., non-causal.

Sometimes, it has been said that in action there is an implicit reference to some set of rules, norms or principles in terms of which the action is described and can be evaluated. Here, the main point is that actions are typically done for certain reasons, and these reasons involve reference to rules, norms, standards or principles. It cannot be denied that values enter into the very description of a large number of human actions. But to give reasons is to show how things will be better for the actions having occurred. Also, to give *justifying* reasons for an action is to do something very different from giving a *causal* explanation of that action. Causal explanation involves citing prior events and laws which correlate those events with subsequent events, whereas explanation in terms of reason involves showing how the action is a case of how things *ought* to be.

Philosophers who assimilate reasons to causes have rightly pointed out certain similarities between the two kinds of explanation. Both cause-explanation and reason-explanation can be signified by the words "because", "cause" and "even reason". But the mere presence of the words, "because", "cause" and "but for" in two explanations does not make them of the same kind. A person's reason for doing X must contain a reference either to X or to something which is thought by the agent to be a means to X. On the other hand, to qualify a phenomenon as a cause, we must observe certain characters that are necessarily the sign of causal relation. Thus, reasons and causes are very different staffs, although in some cases reason does perform the role of cause. If there are good reasons for saying that actions are *caused* by reasons, then the presence of decisions or dispositions does complicate the causal story by introducing a further link in the causal chain. To cite my reasons for acting is to cite those beliefs and desires which were such that I would not have acted that way if I had not them at that particular time. Do we not have here a relationship most naturally classified as a *causal* relationship between these desires and beliefs on the one hand and my action on the other? It would seem that one's reason for doing something must be causally necessary for producing one's action. Since the relation between a cause and its effect is very different from the relation between reasons and actions, we can refute the above suggestive thesis. We shall mention, therefore, three purported differences between "reason action" and "cause-effect" relations: (1) Cause and effect must be *essentially connected* to each other, whereas reasons and actions are not; (2) Cause and effect relationships must be instances of generalizations, whereas reasons actions are not so; and (3) Causal relationship can be known only on the "basis" of previous experiences, whereas one can know the reason's for one's own actions without such evidence.

(1) It is frequently claimed that causes and effects must be logically independent of each other in such a way that the existence or the non-existence of the one must in no way logically entail the existence or non-existence of the other. But as a reply to this view point it might be stated that the cause-effect relation is not a case of a logically-independent relation. A cause is that the occurrence of which is necessary for the occurrence of a thing, i.e. it is necessary and sufficient for the occurrence of a thing. If this is so, then the presence of a cause entails the existence or the non-existence of its corresponding effect. But there is no doubt about the fact that the presence of my reasons for doing some actions in no way entails that the action will occur. "Reason for" is an intentional notion, containing an internal reference to something. Since one's reasons typically consist of one's *beliefs* and *desires* at that time, it should be pointed out that these two are logically independent of actions. In reasoning, man is essentially free; a free person cannot account for the *necessary connection* between his reasons and actions.

(2) When we have a causal explanation, we appeal either explicitly or implicitly to a generalization which links cause and effect by stating that whenever the prior circumstances obtain the event follows. It is evident

that reasons and actions do not meet this condition. Here we do not have a causal connection. Although there may be a simple law connecting reasons and actions, but that must not be identified with causal laws in nature. Following Hempel, it[50] can be said that explanations of human actions are nomological in import at least, if not in explicit formulation. This argument intends to show that the explanandum phenomenon has resulted from certain antecedent and perhaps concomitant conditions and these conditions may concern psychological or sociological tendencies. Hempel shows that reason explanations do not differ in their logical character from explanation in physics or elsewhere. It is instructive to recall Davidson[51] who tries to show that some or other nomic regularity often named as law of nature is at work behind human action. Davidson argues explicitly in favour of the nomological character of causality: "when there is causality there must be a law; events related as cause and effect fall under strict deterministic laws[52]". The only difference between the viewpoints presented by Hempel and Davidson consist in emphasizing the exact manner in which laws are involved when we explain a certain action by mentioning the agent's reasons.

Davidson holds the opinion that the laws that are implicit in reason-explanations seem to concern only individuals. We do have nomic wisdom concerning mankind and womankind but this does not directly enter into reason-explanations. This wisdom advises us about the nature of dispositions such as desires and beliefs. In assessing this theory, we should note that Davidson finds no incompatibility between intention and causality. It is true that action is linked up with the body but actions have an intentional character also. Davidson's theory suffers mainly due to his desire to identify human actions with bodily or physical movements or natural events. As actions are not identical with natural movements, so regularities behind human actions are not nomic regularities which work at the level of physical phenomena. Thus, a generalization connecting reasons and actions might be formulated in the way that whenever a person faces such and such circumstances, he will act in such and such manner. As men are rational, that, particular generalization might not be true of all men. Men are more or less free to decide their courses of actions, make up their mind in given situations and to develop their attitudes differently under different conditions.

3. Another important feature of an ordinary causal relationship seems

to be lacking in the case of reasons and actions. In the ordinary cases, to know that A is the cause of B one must have evidence in the form of analogous cases. But in a good many cases in which an agent acts for a particular reason, we can know what his reason was without the need of experience of analogous cases or any other kinds of influential reasoning. The kind of knowledge one has of one's own reasons in acting is not compatible with the existence of a causal relation between reason and actions. A person knows his own reasons in acting infallibly without induction or observation and no ordinary causal relationship can be realized in this way. Consequently, reasons which explain an action best are all man made, and do not cause the actions that they rationalize.

In philosophy, a distinction has sometimes been drawn between "motives", "intentions", "desires" as referring to quite different things. A man's intention is *what* he aims at or chooses, while his motive is *what* determines his aim or choice. But the present discussion is not concerned with the matter whether or not "motive", "intentions" refer to the same thing rather than whether or not they determine *causally* the doing of an action. We have seen that motives or intentions—which constitute the reasons for human action are not *causally* but *intentionally* necessary for the explanation of human action. It seems that causal explanation is alien to the mode of understanding that we ordinarily seek of human actions.

CHAPTER IV

Causality and Determinism

In this chapter, I propose to develop my arguments in the following order. First, I state the meaning of doctrine—causal determinism, and to make it clear, I intend to answer the question "What does causal determinism assert?" Then I shall discuss whether or not causal determinism is a characteristic of modern science and refer to some specific points made by different thinkers. In the last section of this chapter, I shall conclude my arguments by focussing on the place of the principle of causal determination in modern science.

1. What is Causal Determinism?

Causal determinism is not a new doctrine. It is of great importance in science as well as in everyday life. Different formulations of the doctrine of causal determinism are available, viz., "Everything that has a beginning must have a cause", "Everything has a cause", etc. Causal law always asserts the form of the causal bond, whereas causal determinism asserts that everything happens according to the causal law.

Generally, causation is understood to be synonymous with causal connection. Before we delve further, it will be our task to explicate the status of the category of causation. Is it a form of interdependence, i.e. does it have an ontological status? Or, is it a purely epistemological category solely concerned with our experience and knowledge of things as distinct from the trait or structure of the things themselves? Locke, Berkeley and Hume, among others, regard causation as subjective phenomenon or a mental construct. Locke[53], states that whatever produces any simple or complex idea is denoted by the general name "cause", and that which is produced, is termed "effect". It is a way of interpreting causal category as a category of relation among ideas. In the writings of Berkeley, we find the view that to produce its effect, a cause must be active and this activity involves willing i.e. the only possible cause is a being possessed with *will*, e.g. God makes Him the direct cause of everything. Thus, all causality in nature is traceable to the will-causality (of God); all causality is mind-dependent causality. Hume points out that it is not possible to verify empirically that a definite cause *produces* a definite effect. All that we can say is that an experienced event, i.e. cause is invariably conjoined with another experienced event, i.e. effect. Locke maintains causation to be a *connection* which makes room for production, whereas Hume maintains it as a *relation*, connection being a subclass of relation. Without delving into the criticism of epistemic character of the category of causation that has been made elsewhere by other thinkers, we would merely like to state the opposite thesis, namely causation is *not* a category of relation among *ideas*, but rather, a category of connection and determination of the states of the (factual) world. To hold that causation is an ontological category is to assert that causation is an objective form of inter dependence, obtaining among real events or happenings in nature. As the real connection between the events in the world is not directly known to us, we have to frame a hypothesis, which we shall try to test in the face of relevant findings.

Some thinkers identify "causation" with "determination" and some others take considerable pains to point out the distinction between the two. The word "determination" may mean various things. In its first sense, the word "determination" means something which has definite characteristics. In science, the most frequent use of the word "determination" stands for *constant* and *unique connection* among or between events. If "necessity" is treated as that which is constant and unique in a connection, then the word "determination" amounts to a necessary connection. But, a constant and unique connection between events need not be necessarily causal. Broadly speaking, determinism states that events happen in some definite ways and are, therefore, predictable in accordance with some general laws. But, what are the essential components of all types of determinacy? The essential components of determinacy are according to Mario Bunge[54], productivity and lawfulness, which can adequately characterize the fact of general determinacy. Thus, determinism is a doctrine whose necessary and sufficient conditions are: (1) the genetic principle or the principle of productivity which states that nothing can arise out of nothing or pass into nothing; and (2) the principle of lawfulness which asserts that nothing happens in a lawless fashion. Having conjoined these two statements, we get a third (3) condition, viz., everything is determined (in accordance with laws) by something else, this something being external as well as the internal conditions of the object in question. General determination may be of many kinds, viz., mechanical, structural, teleological, causal, etc. The causal determination being a particular case of determinacy, essentially obtains when the determination of the effect is effected in a unique way by means of its cause. That is to say, causal determinism is but a type of determinism and is subsumed under determinism in general.

According to the Humeans, an essential component of causation is contiguity. It was Hume who not only held the view that the idea of contiguity in space is one of the essential components of the idea of causation but went so far as to assert that it was the first of the component parts of the idea of causation appearing upon an analysis of the latter. Causality is to be primarily defined in terms of contiguity. But it is very difficult to understand why an empiricist should stick fast to the belief that contiguity is not only an essential element but also an indispensable ingredient of a scientific world view, for he himself admits that contiguity is not a fact directly ascertainable by experience but only a useful hypothesis. The hypothesis of contiguity entails an empirically improvable interpolation which is not consistent with the spirit of classical empiricism. In this context, our suggestion is that causation is consistent with contiguity but does not necessarily entail it, nor is entailed by it.

According to many positivists, the concept of causation should be replaced by or actually reduced to invariable succession in time. The identification of causation with invariable succession has been subjected to various criticisms. The fundamental point of criticism is that the reduction of determination to precedence would prevent us from distinguishing the few relevant antecedents in the mass of precedents and would amount to commit the fallacy of *post hoc ergo propter hoc*. The contemporary physicists interpret causality in a more sophisticated manner. In other words, the knowledge of the initial state of a system is sufficient for the production of its state at any other time. But, this formulation is inadequate. Empirical information is never quantitatively exact. The causal problem is chiefly an ontological one. So, causation is not exhausted by regular succession in time, although causal chains may, of course, develop in time in accordance with fixed patterns. That is why the empiricist critique of causality is not at all satisfactory.

The functionalists' critique of causality deserves careful scrutiny. The functionalists claim that causation can indeed be replaced by functional interdependence. Interdependence does not mean an genetic inter-relation but rather, mutual dependence among the existents. Functions are mathematical "forms" that may be filled with infinite contents. The main shortcoming of functionalism is its lack of recognition of the productive genetic character of determination. It is poorer than causation in the sense that it can express a mutual dependence among things or qualities that may coexist without being genetically related to one another. Causal determinism does not mean functional determinism.

The view that causality is fatalistic is inconsistent with causal determinism. This is so, because fatalism is a super naturalistic doctrine and asserts the existence of an unknown destiny, whereas causal determinism can be regarded as a rational theory offering the means for knowing the cause of events. The necessity asserted by fatalism is lawless, whereas causal necessity is lawful. Statements of causal laws assert that if and only if certain conditions are met, a certain result will follow. Therefore, fatalistic determinism should not be confused with causal determinism.

Mechanistic philosophy reduces causality to mechanical causality. But mechanics—whether classical or quantum—is not a purely causal discipline, since it restricts causes to forces. It constitutes a limitation on causality. Mechanics rejects the scholastic maxim that everything that moves is moved by something else and acknowledges the element of spontaneity and, hence, of non-causality. The principle of inertia enunciated by Galileo, Descartes, and Newton is openly non-causal, for it states that a certain type of change requires no external cause to proceed. Classical mechanics contains an important causal ingredient; it has a causal range, e.g. Newton's second law which states "Force causes acceleration" is not a strictly causal law, because it cannot account for the cause of the first motion of the planets around the sun. Thus, causal determinism is something very different from mechanical determinism.

One of the essential conditions for causal determination is the continuity of action between the cause and its effect. It means the absence of gap between the cause and the effect. But we should not forget that the hypothesis of continuity has a very wide but limited domain of validity. If causal chains are valid in limited contexts, it is because they "reflect" reality, maybe in an abstract way, i.e. there is a sort of structural resemblance between the real world and the causal chain.

The other characteristic of the principle of causal determination is that it asserts a one-sided dependence of the effect upon the cause, i.e. it reflects the cause-effect direction which means it asserts activity and neglects passivity. The unidirectional nature attributed to the causal nexus is consistent with the empiricist doctrine of uniform, unique succession of events. But we have already seen that a regular time series and uniquely determined series may (but need not) necessarily be causal.

Scientifically speaking, causal determination is external determination. Causality is undoubtedly a theory of change. But does it mean a radical change? To this question, two answers are possible. The first is that causes can bring forth novelty. According to the other, what can be regarded as the strict doctrine of causality has often been rejected just against the possibility of the emergence of newness. There are a number of thinkers who believe that the process of causation can give rise to objects which are new only in number or in quantity but not in kind. This formulation excludes novelty and asserts two things: (1) the effect includes the same as the cause; and (2) the effect contains less than the cause. This is the teaching of the Sāṃkhya thinkers in Indian philosophy as well in the writings of Aristotle. Aristotle holds the view that change is the growth or manifestation of pre-existing potentialities. Kant also adopted a qualitatively unchangeable picture of the universe. He asserts that causation is a form of pure thought, a category belonging to the conceptual canvas on which human experience is pointed. A new-Kantian has observed that the true meaning of causal law is that there is nothing new in the world. The principle of the conservation of energy and the principle of the conservation of electric charge are to be regarded as expressions of causal laws. The world remains the same, meaning therby that the cause is just the form taken previously by the effect and the effect is the form that the cause takes. It is by means of law statements that scientific descriptions of change—whether qualitative or quantitative— are achieved. Laws are modes of being and becoming and as such relate entities. Thus, causation definitely excludes novelty by declaring that the actuals are either the new manifestation or the qualitative development of possibles. And, if it be the case, we are faced with a strange situation, viz., the doctrine of causality which is supposed to account for change ends by denying radical change. The problem of novelty is not insolvable as imagined by other thinkers. Whereas the principle "Same cause same effect" does not appear to hold good, we tend to assume that the cause has not been the *same* in *all* cases, i.e. something new emerges unnoticed. Causation participates in the production of novelty but it does not exhaust it.

Causality was the most general defining character of modern science from its beginning till the birth of quantum mechanics. But most philosophers think that the causal concept is much older than modern science. Of the several branches of physics, the first contains all the laws of classical physics, such as the conservation of energy and the law of gravitation. The laws are stated to be universal. The second department of physics is concerned with large aggregates and the laws of chance, the laws stated to be widely *probable*. The third department of physics, i.e. quantum theory is the most disturbing of all, since it seems to show that the law of causality cannot be applied to the doings of individual electrons.

Classical mechanics or Newtonian mechanics is the generally acknowledged paradigm of a deterministic theory. Viewed quite generally, mechanics is a set of equations that formulate the dependence of certain traits of bodies on other physical properties. Mechanics studies the relation between a large number of properties belonging to a certain type of class. S is a deterministic system with respect to the properties in K if, and only if, the state of S at any given time uniquely determines its state at any other time. This is the rough abstract model of illustrating the sense in which classical mechanics is a deterministic theory. Laplace is simply expounding the deterministic nature of mechanics. But attempts have been made to eliminate the sources of possible misconceptions concerning the sense in which mechanics is itself a deterministic thesis. What mechanics can predict is only *a class* of values which must not be unique set of values. Rather, these are good approximation to a theoretical state of a system. Yet it is true that before Newton, there existed no self-contained system of physical causality which was capable of representing any of the deeper features of the empirical world. There is no doubt about the fact that the gradual revolution in our fundamental notions has taken place since the end of the nineteenth century. Theoretical physics has outgrown the Newtonian frame which gave stability and intellectual guidance for nearly two hundred years. Einstein himself modifies[55] Newton's theory. In spite of these modifications, according to Newton's system, all happenings are to be interpreted mechanically, i.e. as motions of material points according to Newton's law of motion. Since causal determinism does not necessarily mean mechanical determinism, the primary question raised is: what is the precise sense in which the theories of classical physics are deterministic while current subatomic theory is not.

It has often been alleged in recent years that there is at least one branch of physics in which the principle of adequacy of mechanical causality breaks down. Having this allegation in the back of our mind, let us new consider the place of this principle in one of the most modern departments of science, i.e. quantum mechanics. This theory, concerned with individual behaviour of atoms and electrons, is still in a process of development and far from its final form. In the hands of Heisenberg, it has received a more disturbing and revolutionary interpretation. The most perplexing thing about it is that it raises serious doubt about the universality of causality; at least that is how it has often been understood. Eddington goes so far as to believe that perhaps the atoms have a certain amount of free will and their behaviour is not wholly subject to law. There is what is known as the "principle of indeterminacy", which says that a particle may have position or velocity but cannot have both in an exactly calculable or predictable way. This is interpreted by some thinkers as a breakdown of physical determinism. The principle of indeterminacy was introduced by Heisenberg on the grounds that it is impossible to determine with precision both the position and the momentum of a particle. There will be a margin of error in each, and the product of the two errors is constant. It means that the more accurately we determine the one, the less accurately we shall be determining the other and *vice versa*.

It is interesting to see how the champions of the uncertainty relation vacillate between a subjective approach and an objective one. The first states that the particle has an exact position and an exact momentum but it is impossible to measure them both simultaneously. The other possible interpretation asserts that it is inadmissible to attribute to the particle anything like a sharp "position–cum–momentum;" it simply has no path. Russell declares that there is no good reason for supposing that the behaviour of the sub–atomic particles is not subject to laws and it is no wonder if the laws of the behaviour have not yet been discovered. Einstein is inclined to the opinion that a physicist, in the long run, will not content themselves with this sort of indirect description of the real. We may not know the exact cause of everything but as a matter of fact, all actions proceed from external as well as from internal necessity. That is to say, the rational or the real structure of the world is completely determined. Russell and Einstein tried to prove that the indeterminism of quantum physics is subjective. In future, equipped with better methods and instruments, we shall be able to determine the position and velocity of an electron simultaneously with absolute accuracy. This way of thinking, as we all know, is common in layman. When philosophy refuses to settle its account with the new findings of science, it ceases to be critical and dogmatic.

It has been pointed out by some philosophers that the implication of the principle of indeterminacy has often been mystified and seriously misunderstood. Ayer[56], for example, argues that the validity of the principle of determinism has been disputed by philosophers for the wrong reasons. In dealing with the "principle of uncertainty", it is important not to make the mistake of supposing that the uncertainty relations show that there is anything indeterminate in nature. The principle does not purport to prove the absence of order in sensible occurrences themselves; it only points out the inadequacy of the conceptual scheme into which classical physics have tried to fit in those occurrences. Ayer's interest is to establish the view that if there is to be any reason for believing in the law of universal causation, it must be based upon our actual observations of the occurrences of sensible events. The number of universal laws which are good inductive grounds for believing are sufficiently great to make it highly probable that every event is connected with some other event in such a way that one can infer its occurrence from the known occurrence of the other event by means of a valid causal or even a valid statistical law. Thus, the principle of causal determination cannot be treated rigorously as the principle of explanation in the most modern department of science.

Given the quantum theory in its present form, Moritz Schlick[57], among others, also rules out the possibility of giving a strictly deterministic description of nature. The real reason of the rejection of determinism is primarily that it is impossible to predict phenomena with perfect accuracy. This is the inevitable consequence of Heisenberg's famous indeterminacy principle. In this connection, Schlick argues that the physicists emphasize the impossibility not of the prediction of future states but of the complete description of the present state of a physical system. In spite of all these consequences, Schlick believes in the practical significance of the principle of determination. For all ordinary purposes of science and everyday life, the deterministic attitude is compatible with our knowledge of nature. Otherwise, the principle of indeterminacy would make our life very difficult. Recent development in quantum mechanics logically proves the inapplicability of the principle of determination in a particular field of nature, whereas for all practical purposes of science, it is essential. Schlick upholds the objective approach about the uncertainty relation. But the manner of his defence of determinism from the narrow practical point of view is indefensible. If objective indeterminism constitutes the truth of nature, then no scientist can fulfil the task of discovering the laws for predictions.

Heisenberg, who formulated "the principle of indeterminacy", believed in objective indeterminism. Heisenberg holds the view that what prevents modern physics from retaining causality is the impossibility of simultaneously measuring exact values of conjugate variables, such as the position and the momentum of a "particle". This, in turn, prevents us from formulating accurate predictions about the future states of the "particle". The rigorous formulation of the causal principle runs thus; if we know the present exactly, we may calculate the future exactly. But the point is that in principle, we can never know the present exactly in details; the antecedent of the proposition can never come true. This comparative uncertainty in the prediction of the results of measurement is an empirical indeterminacy which by no means warrants the validity of indeterminism in an ontological, i.e. realistic sense. But it is not an unbound indeterminacy. The uncertainty is not the reflection of an objective indeterminateness, of a lack of precise connection between the successive states of micro-physical systems because it refers to the results of measurement and not to things in themselves. Ontological determinism is consistent with epistemological "Probabilism". The principle of indeterminacy is concerned with the measurement and not with causations. There is nothing in the principle of indeterminacy to show that every physical event is uncaused. Thus, the uncertainty principle cannot serve the purpose of proving the breakdown of causal determinism in quantum mechanics.

2. The Place of the Principle of Causal Determination in Modern Science

The chief theoretical aim of scientific research is to answer the questions beginning with what, where, when, why, etc. Linguistic formulations apart, what the scientists really strive after is to solve problems and explain otherwise unintelligible situations in terms of general laws, including causal ones. It is commonly believed that with the help of scientific laws, all questions—how, why, etc., are answerable. We have seen that scientific laws may be of different types, for scientific research does not dispense entirely with the concept of cause and science contains both causal and non-causal laws. Many empiricists claim that the concept of cause can be replaced by that of law, i.e. behind every law a causal connection is to be sought. Since science is concerned with causal as well as non-causal laws, that particular claim cannot be upheld. The present trend in science shows a diversification of the type of scientific law, along side an increasing realization that several categories of determination contribute to the production of every real event. The test of scientific research is not the stage of formulating causal laws. What it attempts to show is that here questions are answered in terms not only of causes but of several categories of determination. Newton realized that the fundamental function of scientific discovery of the laws of phenomena—whether or not the causal aspect is prominent in them. It only means that causal determination is not the only form of determination. Scientific laws are the chief tools of scientific explanation of nature, thought and society.

To explain means literally to unfold, expose or develop. Scientific explanation consists in showing that the proposition stating the fact is a consequence of one or more proposition of greater generality. But logic does not tell us the whole story of knowledge. In order to complete the picture of a scientific explanation, we have to look at its ontological aspect. In our attempt to ascertain whether a given explanation is causal or not, its logical framework is not only insufficient but also partly irrelevant.

This can be done only by deciding the ontological features of the explanan—propositions. Further, an ontological emphasis upon current types of scientific explanation has shown that there are many ways of answering why questions, one of them being the means of causes. It is the peculiarity of scientific explanation in general that it is to be framed in terms of laws and some of these laws have a causal component while others lack it.

Prediction is essential to test a scientific hypothesis, and to see whether it is causal or not. Prediction, according to some thinkers, constitutes the touchstone of the factual adequacy of theories. It is also a general assumption that causal laws formulate predictions with certainty. But this is not true. The success of a prediction depends on a host of factors, and there is always a source of error in the limited precision with which the specific information is available. Predictability is not the meaning of causation but a criterion of both causal and non-causal hypotheses. Successful prediction enables us to confirm or invalidate scientific law statements—whether causal or not. The failure to predict by way of a law with a strong causal component does not invalidate the law in every respect. This failure proves that the principle has no universal validity and, consequently, does not entail complete indeterminacy in the real world.

The above considerations help us to formulate our view regarding the place of the principle of causal determination in modern science. The causal principle, as one of the various important categories of determination, enjoys an approximate validity in limited ranges. Strict and pure causation works nowhere. The principle of causal determination is only partially active, that too only in certain cases. Its task is to inform us that reality is not a chaotic aggregate of isolated events; rather, events are produced and conditioned in different ways. Consequently, the principle of causal determination as a general principle enjoys only an approximate validity within a limited domain.

CHAPTER V

Causality and Freedom

In the course of analysis, I shall further try to define the highly controversial relation between causality and freedom. Our analysis of causality would otherwise, remain incomplete. In this chapter, my objective is to try to answer mainly two questions: (a) what is the true antithesis of freedom? Cause, or external constraint? (b) Can the realm of freedom be shown to be logically continuous with that of causality? Where do, if at all, causality and freedom meet?

The dispute concerning "freedom of the will" consists in its advocate's attempt to refute and its opponent's attempt to establish the validity of the causal principle in relation to human will. Though the exact relation between the concept of freedom and the concept of causality is not always made clear, the argument runs thus: if anything that happens has a cause, then we live in a causal universes. In other words, causalism is true; and if causalism be true, there would be no room for man's free will. Facing two and only two alternatives, man must choose one of them—either there is freedom and, therefore, causal determination is false, or causal determination is a fact, and, hence, there is no freedom.

It has often been claimed that sciences—in so far as they try to explain certain events, whether these be human actions or physical occurrences—must assume the principle of causality and their task is to make predictions about up coming events. It is true that factors operating on man are far more complex than factors giving rise to a natural occurrence and, therefore, far more difficult to discover but in kind, the former are the same as the latter ones. And we know far more today than ever before about, for example, people's hereditary conditions, the laws of how people behave, all the factors that make people act as they do; and consequently, man is becoming more and more like the stone. This is the view of the opponents of free-will doctrine.

The advocates of the free-will doctrine try to establish the point that freedom is the main postulate of morality. If causal determination holds good everywhere—as the determinist claims—i.e. if all events obey immutable laws then my will too is always determined by innate character and motives. Hence, my decisions are necessary and not free. If the case be so, then I am not responsible for "my" acts, for I would be accountable for them only if I could do something about the way my decisions want; but I can do nothing about it, since they proceed necessarily from my character and the motives. The motives come from without and my character is the necessary product of the innate tendencies and external influences. Thus, causal determinism is not compatible with moral responsibility, which presupposes a freedom that is an exemption from causality. Let us analyze the meanings of the highly ambiguous term "freedom".

1. Freedom

Following Adler,[58] we may distinguish three different uses of the term "freedom"—circumstantial, acquired and natural. The terms "circumstantial", "acquired" and "natural" are used to signify three distinct modes of possession, i.e. three distinct ways in which freedom is thought of as belonging to man. Freedom is "circumstantial" if and only if it consists in an individual's ability to act according to his wishes. A man is free when he possesses the power to abstain from an intended action, when his actions are under his control. A man acts under compulsion when he is forced to do a thing unintended by him. Empiricist philosophers such as Hume, Mill, Schlick and others believe in circumstantial freedom. Again, some philosophers think that there is an ideal of freedom which we all aspire after but only a few achieve. Acquired freedom means an individual's ability to live as he ought to. Rationalist thinkers, Spinoza and Leibnitz for example, also hold this view. But this view of freedom should not be confused with that of freedom of decision, and the question at issue is the freedom of choice. The advocates of the theory of "natural" freedom believe that freedom is inherent in all human beings regardless of the circumstances under which they live and without regard to any state of mind, which they may or may not acquire in the course of their lives. Kant, however, makes freedom natural by making a sharp distinction between two realms—in one of these realms determinism holds and in the other it does not.

The word "freedom" is used to mean different modes of having and exercizing of power. Whether or not these different meanings can significantly characterize man's freedom of will is a question to be decided later on. At present, our task would be to search for the common issue presented in all ordinary usages of the word "freedom". It is a fact that human actions are marked by the freedom of decision. Harold Ofstad[59] has rightly pointed out six main ways of using the sentence "P decided freely in the situation S".

(a) P's decision in S was not subject to compulsion.

(b) P's decision in S was not determined.

(c) P's decision in S expressed his self.

(d) P's decision in S was a rational decision.

(e) P, in S, decided as he ought to.

(f) P—in S decided—has it in his power to decide otherwise than he did.

Each of the above formulations needs further elaboration. But all of them centre around one common issue: the question of our power to decide. In conceiving freedom as the absence of compulsion, one posits compulsion as the most serious obstacle to the exercise of power. In conceiving the "free" as "the uncaused", one emphasizes on the point that denial of causation guarantees the exercize of man's power. Thus, the common issue underlying different approaches to the problem of the freedom of decision is the question of man's power to decide.

2. Antitheses of Freedom

(i) Constraint Physical or Natural

Philosophers who believe that nature constitutes an obstacle to man's power to decide otherwise hold the view that the real antithesis of freedom is external constraint. Empiricist philosophers, in general, seem to uphold such a view.

Hume holds[60] the opinion that men have always agreed both in the doctrine of necessity and in the doctrine of liberty, the terms "necessity" and "liberty" taken in reasonable senses. Hume states that we know nothing further of causation than merely the constant conjunction of objects (which comprise physical events as well as human actions and mental states like motives, volitions), and the mind—in inferring the one from the other—imagines things to be necessarily connected. Its imagination, however, is backed by custom or habit. Necessity or its opposite are not predicates of things but predicates ascribed by thought on things due to its inherent propensity. The necessity of an action, whether of matter or of mind, consists in the determination of the thoughts of the person who considers that action, to infer the existence of that action from some preceding objects. Liberty, as opposed to necessity, is nothing but the lack of this determination and a certain looseness which we feel in passing or not passing from the idea of one object to the idea of another object which succeeds the former. Hume's point is that when we analyse "actions of mind" or human actions, we never come across any such absence of determination or the presence of looseness. We imagine that we are at liberty in translating our will into action and forget precisely the point that the will as the motive of actions is under constraint. Hume says "...however we may *imagine* we feel a liberty within ourselves, a spectator can commonly infer our actions from our motives and character; and even when cannot, he includes in general, that he might, were he perfectly acquainted with *every circumstance of our situation and temper*, and the most secret springs of our complexion and disposition. Now this is the very essence of necessity..............[61]"

Our main objection to Hume is that the condition which he lays down for declaring an act of mind to be physically necessary is forever unattainable for us and this is unattainable not merely in practice but also in principle. Neither any external observer nor I myself can completely explore or control my situation. Under Hume's phenomenalistic-analysis, self identify turned out to be a theoretical fiction. Consciousness, for Hume, was a unidimensional flow. But we believe that consciousness is essentially intentional, that is object-encountering. The intentionality of our consciousness is such an immediate phenomenon that my present "I" cannot tell what my future "I" will do or be. Generalizations about past intentions of their own account cannot shed light on my future unless past intentions are chosen by me as reasons for my future actions. Due to the bottomlessness of my consciousness, neither I nor any external observer of my behaviour can predict my choice, though it should be admitted that I enjoy a priviledged access to my own mind which others do not. This, however, does not mean solipsism because we give due recognition to the fact in making a choice we are influenced, among other things, by our situations—the self other dialectic is a never-ending process.

Though Mill[62] does not state like Hume that the source of the controversy between the doctrine of necessity and the doctrine of freedom is a linguistic difficulty, he also firmly asserts that the controversy is based on certain misconceptions. Mill declares that though he is an upholder of the doctrine of necessity, he is no necessitarian. And necessarianism—thinks Mill—logically culminates in fatalism which states that it is of no use to struggle against what is about to happen, for we cannot prevent its happening by our efforts. In other words, the necessitarian believes that his nature is formed *for* him, and not *by* him; therefore his desire to change his character is of no use. Mill criticizes the necessitarian on the score that even if we grant that ultimately a person's nature in formed *for* him, we do not see how it is compatible with the view that his nature is partly formed by him as one of its intermediate agents. Mill thinks that "philosophical necessity" operates in the realm of physical events as well as in the realm of human actions. If we can know the motives, dispositions, and character of a person, we can accurately infer the way in which he will act and if we knew all the inducements a person is subject to, we could foretell his conduct just as we could predict the physical events. Also, this does not hamper our feeling of freedom because we possess a limited awareness of our dispositions and inclinations. As Mill discovers an analogy between mental acts and physical events in so far as both are "caused" (constantly preceded or followed) events, we do not see how he can save the feeling of freedom unless the feeling is interpreted as mere fancy. Even if we, unlike the necessitarian, include the agent's desire to mould his character as an intermediate factor within the set of total circumstances determining the person's character, that desire itself, being a mental event, would be in its turn caused and as such predictable in principle at least. And, in that case, we do not see how freedom can be saved.

A.J. Ayer[63] has pointed out the fact that freedom is to be contrasted not with causality but with constraint. What exactly is meant by constraint?

A person may be compelled by some person or forced to do what, left to himself, he would not have done and, in that case, his action would not be moral. Ayer says that in performing an act, which we are compelled to perform, we are not free. If it is true that we choose to follow a particular course of action rather than another, there must be some causal explanation of this choice though the cause in terms of which we seek to explain it is of a very special sort. It is not the case that we are not free when our actions are caused. Being constrained to do an action entails being caused to do it but being caused to do it does not necessarily entail being constrained to do it. Ayer's way of defining compulsion as a kind of causality is a way of arguing for the causal explanation of human actions and this does not fully describe the problem situation. Ayer is right in viewing that a person's decision is not a matter of pure chance but he seems to be wrong in thinking that the denial of the accidental character of choice does not necessarily entail the purely causal character of a choice. Sometimes we choose immediately for which no causal explanation can be offered. Thus, to make our free choices rational, does not mean to make them essentially causal.

Schlick contends[64] that the relation which causal laws bear to human willingness is very different from the "compulsive" relation which prescriptive less bear to it. Causal laws are *descriptive* laws; they describe what does always happen. *Prescriptive* laws, however, are also imposed by some civil authority and these may fairly be said to exercize compulsion. Upholder of the traditional doctrine, according to Schlick, confused descriptive with prescriptive laws. The only freedom implied by moral responsibility is freedom from compulsion. The consciousness of responsibility is the consciousness of freedom, which is merely the knowledge of having acted out of one's own desires. And "one's own desires" are those which have their origin in the regularity of one's character in the given situation and are not imposed by external power. The absence of external power finds its expression in the well-known feeling that one could have acted otherwise if we willed something else. What is important is that this feeling is not the consciousness of the absence of a cause, but of something altogether different, namely, freedom.

Freedom is contrasted with external constraint which prevents us from translating our desires into action. The true meaning of the question, "Have we free will?" is simply "can we translate our desires into actions?"

The answer is, "sometimes we can and sometimes we cannot, depending upon the specific circumstances of the case". Schlick's account of the compatibility between freedom and causality holds good only if we grant that the translation of desires into action is necessarily causal. But we cannot grant this ideology. Human mind is essentially free and active. Schlick does not appear to be quite aware of the fact that there might be a connection between a person's desire and his action, which need not be construed as causal. Consequently, Schlick's attempt to reconcile causality with freedom does not make much headway.

On the above question, Russell's[65] opinion is noteworthy. He says that while deciding, we enjoy a subjective sense of freedom. This subjective sense of freedom consists in our to choose from a number of alternatives. But this does not show that there is no causal connection between what we want to choose and our previous history. It would be a paradox to say that a man's decision ought not to be influenced by his belief as to what is his duty. If he is allowed to decide an act in a particular way because he believes it to be his duty, his decision has a motive, i.e. cause, and, he is not free in the sense in which the determinist must deny the freedom. Russel is right in thinking that an action is influenced by motive, intention, etc., but he is wrong in holding that there is a causal connection between the two. The question: how far human actions are subject to causal laws? is important. Every mental event is a genuine novelty and not predictable from the previous events—this contention has a great deal of truth in it. But Russell attempts to overcome the trouble by suggesting that there are precisely the same kinds of reason for regarding it as probable that they all have causes as there are in the case of physical events. Is it a tenable suggestion? Perhaps not. The sense in which there is a constant relation between causes of certain *kinds* and effects of certain *kinds* in the case of natural events is completely different from the sense in which there is a constant relation between the causes of free actions. Human actions are so marked by novelty that no theoretical prediction is possible about them. Therefore, a Russellian attempt to reconcile causality with freedom by maintaining an opposition between freedom and constraint cannot be accepted as satisfactory. It is true that there obtains an important distinction between causal laws and compulsive laws but it is quite erroneous to think that compulsive laws *always* limits human freedom. A man can be free to do what he likes in spite of being constrained. Apart from this, the idea of "external constraint" is very ambiguous, i.e. it depends upon a man's power, ability, ideas, etc. There cannot be "universal compulsion". So, its opposition with freedom is always peculiar to peculiar situations and that, in its own, is insignificant.

Now it is necessary to clearly spell out the main contentions of the above-mentioned empiricists. There are thinkers who mark these philosophers as "soft determinists". Broadly speaking, these philosophers do not believe any inconsistency whatever between the doctrine of determinism and the doctrine that human beings are sometimes free agents. When we call an action free, we mean that it is uncaused, and this emphatically includes the kind of action about which we pass moral judgments. By calling an action "free", the empiricists mean that the agent was not compelled to perform it. Sometimes, people act out of certain threats and, in such cases, human actions are not free actions. And, on other occasions, men act in certain ways because of their own rational interests. Thus, in distinguishing between free and unfree actions we do not try to mark the presence and the absence of concerned causes but attempt to indicate the *kind* of causes that are present. But is this position reasonable? We think not. For, we may easily imagine a man who seems to be under constraint from outside, but left to himself, does not feel constrained at all. Therefore, we should forcus our attention on the constrained, i.e. the person under constraint, and not the constraint itself. Secondly, freedom, as conceived by the empiricists, cannot in any way be shown to be compatible with the causal character of human actions. If freedom constitutes the very essence of human mind, it is a dream of the determinists that given any action we can point out the motive or intention with which the action is causally connected.

To this theory, one might say that the conception of *causing* something to happen is the conception of somebody freely making something to happen. Black[66] for example, intends to develop such a view. But what is the case of "making something happen"? A man, for instance, is thirsty, but there is a glass of water within his easy reach and he stretches out his hand, brings the glass nearer and drinks. This is what Black calls a perfect case of making something happen. And, to make something happen is to cause something happen. In order to clarify the situation, Black finds out the following assertions that can be referred to that action.

(i) What happened was made to happen by the person who moved the glass.

(ii) What the person made to happen was the motion of the object moved.

(iii) The person made this happen by *doing* something.

(iv) In doing, the action the person acted freely.

(v) The action occurred throughout the time the motion was occurring.

(vi) The motion would not have occurred unless the action had occurred.

(vii) When the action occurred, the motion had to occur.

The above seven assertions, according to Black, tend to show that the cause was a *free act* of a person, and the effect was a motion of an inanimate object, i.e. a necessary consequence of the cause. So, the assertion that the agent acted freely may be contrasted with forced action. And, since there is no scope for compulsion or inducement in the given case, for, the person looked the glass he "just wanted to", so Black is entitled to add that the very same situation is a clear case and a paradigm for acting freely. We have no objection to the view that no scientific elaboration of the antecedent of the paradigmatic episode could destroy its character as paradigm for acting freely. But what we fail to understand is this: How to treat the free act of a person as a *cause* of the motion of the object? A cause is that which is necessary and sufficient for the occurrence of a thing. The given situation proves that the motion of the object is the result of man's free decision. This further means that the said motion is *produced* by the freedom of action. But mere productivity cannot constitute the essence of causality. If that be the case, then there cannot be a significant distinction between the cases of "happenings" and the cases of "doings". But as a matter of fact, there is a distinction marked by the power of possessing free will as far as "doings" are concerned. This freedom of will, because of its power to do what we like to do, cannot *cause* something to happen; uniqueness remains altogether absent in this performance. Consequently, Black's line of reasoning, far from resolving the conflict between freedom and causality, upholds it.

(ii) Constraint: The Absolute Will

The failure of the empiricists' position stated above has led us to examine the view of these thinkers who opine that submission to a law which is expressive of the will of God and which is absolute in character constitutes an obstacle to man's power to decide freely. Rationalist philosophers (classical) in general seem to defend such a view.

Spinoza[67], for instance, an acosmist of the stronger blend, realizes that there was no sharp distinction between metaphysics and ethics. Also, as the realm of things was, for him, a realm governed by strict necessity, so also was the realm of actions. Human imagines themselves free because they believe that their actions are results of their volitions and desires; but they never dream, in their ignorance, of the causes which have disposed them so to wish and desire. Men are mistaken in thinking themselves free; and this opinion consists of this alone, that they are conscious of their actions and ignorant of the causes by which they are determined. This, therefore, is their idea of liberty that they should know no cause of their action. Thus, men who claim that they posses freedom of will, are conscious of their own desires but ignorant about the causes of such desires. The feeling that the will is uncaused signify nothing more than our lack of comprehension about the operative context in which a decision is taken. Thus, Spinoza can explicitly speak of man as "seeking" means which should lead him to perfection and "striving" to acquire a better nature because, to him, freedom was the recognition of absolute and strict necessity. To the extent man realizes that his emotion is necessitated or ultimately caused by God, he becomes free from its grip. "Seeking" and "striving", which are forms of conduct, are almost synonymous with broadening one's viewpoint and the gap between practical reason and pure reason—doing and knowing—is much more narrowed. But the situation in which an agent acts never comes to him as an objective determination; the agent shapes his situation by his ideas, prejudices, biases and value commitments. The situation or circumstance in which human consciousness feels morally obliged, discovers and rediscovers itself, is open to alternative descriptions. For a monist like Spinoza, ultimately speaking, there is only one situation; the situation viewed under the aspect of eternity and this situation is open to a fixed discription. We believe, however, that the eternal viewpoint which he speaks of, is forever unattainable for finite man who views things "*sub specie temporis*".

Leibnitz offers[68] a somewhat similar argument to define the point that no fact can be found real or existing, no statement true, unless there be a sufficient reason why it should be so and not otherwise. So, he says that in actions, our will is determined by moral necessity, i.e. by the inclination which arises from its recognition of the best, however perfect or imperfect that recognition may be. Our will moves in accordance with our ideals which are nothing but our perception, the potentialities of our nature. Freedom consists in spontaneity and intelligence and intelligence includes every degree of perception. There is an infinite variety of degrees in freedom and no actual concrete substance is subject to an absolutely pure necessity. A human action is free in proportion to the clearness and distinctness of the reasons which determine it. Leibnitz concludes that no human action is undetermined as none is absolutely necessitated. God is the freest of beings and the final cause of all things. This means that man's will is determined by a kind of necessity and this necessity rests ultimately on the nature of God and the Absolute as perfect in wisdom, goodness and power. But as far as a man's free decision is concerned, it can be argued that there cannot be any room for man's free will in the significant sense in Leibnitz's line of reasoning. It is a very tall metaphysical claim that human volitions, intentions, ideas can all be explained exclusively in terms of causal determination. As a matter of fact, we vacillate between different courses of actions and it is not clear to us what would be the explanation of this vacillation unless there be a scope for alternative courses of human actions? In this context, Blanshard's[69] remark is very interesting. He says that every action is caused, but the causes differ in levels; mental causation is not like the clash of billiard balls. But the admission of causal levels shows that Blanshard is a determinist in a Pickwickian sense. In essence, it is a theory which thinks of man as solely a part of nature. But the language of determinism is always dangerous when we are describing, choosing, reasoning and it is better to avoid. In choosing, a man is more or less self determined. Man's life begins on the natural plane, but he is potentially spirit as well. The realm of mind may be a realm of law too, but it is not—as in nature—a law that is invariably obeyed. Also, it is not a law imposed and operative from without; it is a law accepted by mind itself. Everything in nature works in accordance with laws, whereas man determines himself by his consciousness of law. It is this self consciousness which makes it possible for man to regulate his life. It is not an answer to say that if a choice is caused by thought that thought is caused by another and *so on ad infinitum.* Thoughts do not cause one another in only intelligible sense of the word in which the heat *causes* expansion. We do not live in a purely natural life and the failure to realize this is the weakness of the stated view.

The above analysis makes it sufficiently clear why God or Absolute does not constitute the proper antithesis of human freedom. It is now our task to consider the other side of the problem, viz., human actions too are "behaviouristic". This is another may of arguing for the theory that the concept of volition is an artificial concept. Ryle[70], for instance, tries to expose the myth of volitions by delivering a frontal attack on the inner/outer dichotomy as applied to action. Ryle objects to this terminology on the ground that if we speak *both* of a man's overt doings *and* of the volitions they express and also argue that it is the business of the moral philosopher to pass from former to the latter, we set him an impossible task since the volitions here spoken of are, by definition, private to the person who has them and accessible to no one else. In doing so, we involve ourselves in the traditional philosophical problem of our knowledge of other minds, a problem which cannot be solved satisfactorily for the simple reason that it rests on a gross misunderstanding. If we will only recognize that overt intelligent performances are not clues to the workings of minds; they are those workings, then misunderstandings and problems disappear together. The so-called "mental processes" as "acts of volition", Ryle argues, are not in the least like "processes". In this case, none of the ordinary ways of describing processes is applicable: it is useless to ask whether volitions are continuous or interrupted, how they can be speeded up or slowed down, when they begin and when they end. The difference between voluntary and involuntary behaviour does not lie in the fact that voluntary behaviour is preceded, whereas involuntary behaviour is not preceded by an "act of volition". In determining the logical geography of mental conduct concepts, we find that it is a categorical-mistake to suppose that the concept "volition" names any entity whatsoever. The function of the word is to describe human behaviour, not to name an entity.

Ryle's logical behaviourism (informal logical behaviourism if we are allowed to use the term) differs from the older philosophy on two scores. First, it does not indulge in the Hobbesian (or democritusean) blunder of reducing mind to body; this would have shown that there is something as the category of mind to be reduced in the category of body. Secondly, it is not psychological behaviourism of Watson or Woodworth or Hull; categorical distinction was drawn in language, not in reality. The formation rules and as well as the behaviour-governing-rules of mental-category words and physical-category words are not intertranslatable. The question is: are we to explain this absence of inter translatability by rules alone? Is the fact of being a mental word or not being a mental word merely rule-governed; has it no metaphysical load? We cannot say, "the table is kind" but we can very well say "the girl is kind". Is it merely a question of conformity to rules? Is there not something in the identity of the table which makes it impossible for the table to be kind? Is there not something in the identity of the girl which makes it possible for the girl to be kind? We say that the girl has the power to be kind, the table has not. And this brings us to the problem of disposition. Positivistic thesis may be stated thus: actual phenomena are all that are possible. This strains our credibility. We never remain confined within the total actuality but always pass beyond the given to the non-given which is intentionally connected with the given, due to a transcendental affiliation. The language philosopher's interest in trying to understand the use of a word in the various contexts of ordinary language is understandable but, at the same time, we should realize that the *anthropos* possesses a metaphysical or, one may say natural tendency or propensity to search for a common element among details. Man cannot rest content encountering the blind manifold as blind; he feels a rational obligation to systematize, organize, or conceptualize "the given". Wittgenstein, too, acknowledged the generalizing tendency by introducing the concept of family resemblance. Thus, the language-philosopher's analysis does not make much progress to the problem at issue.

(iii) Constraint: Sociological or Historical

The inadequacy of the classical rationalist's interpretation of the antithesis of freedom leads us to consider the view which has recently gained ground is that social life or history constitutes the real contrast of a man's power to decide otherwise. Marx[71] advocates this position. It is the basic contention of Marxist philosophy that all the phases of human life can be adequately explained by reference to the material conditions of that life. Since man is a product of the material world and since all his ideas, thoughts and volitions are ultimately reflections of movements which occur in that world, the material conditions of life must exercise decisive influence on the entire structure of human society and every change in those material conditions will inevitably lead to a transformation of the social structure. We can say that the Marxist theory of historical interpretation is philosophical in so far as it presents its main contention not as a mere empirical hypothesis, but as something much more like an a *priori* truth. But it is futile to attempt to anticipate what the mind will do in future by tracing the past history of the material world in the midst of which it has made its appearance. The theory of historical materialism fails to give a rational interpretation of human history, since it does not take into account the essential nature of human mind and ignores the role which it really plays in shaping that history. To treat man as a being whose moral life is determined for him entirely by social conditions and material goods is to deny the basic character of human freedom. The truth is that self-conscious intelligent individuals, varying their modes of production in accordance with their changing needs, have gradually modified the economic structure of society and have also brought about other related changes. So it is not in economic terms or social conditions alone that all states of affairs must finally be understood. And, if Marx says that it an a *priori* proposition, not an empirical truth, then he must attempt a philosophical justification of it; and this he entirely fails to do.

But there is a view according to which whatever happens in the "life" of society or history is intrinsically rational and we fail to realize this rationality because we do not, or rather cannot, "see" those happenings in their "proper" perspective. Once we cannot accept this view that whatever happens is rational, the only task we are left with is to discover the "proper perspectives" with reference to which the rationality of the happenings in question would become obvious and the laws which govern them. This view has been advocated by Hegel[72]. His view is that consciously or unconsciously, all of us—determined by the cunning of Reason—are moving towards the goal of Reason. This view of historical process and events is extremely deterministic and as such it leaves no room for free will. It seems that the actions of individuals are to be explained by "an internal unchangeable principle" that permeates the entire control of history. In terms of this view, one cannot draw a significant line of distinction between intended and unintended actions of individuals. This is a curious position which permits everything and prohibits nothing, fails to account for the individual's responsibility and also his power to decide otherwise. Hegel identifies the free with the self contained or self sufficient and he found this condition fulfilled not in the individual but in society. To think that man can be moral within the state is to believe in the concept of "freedom in". But Hegel shifted to the concept of "freedom to" in declaring that the freeest expression of man demands his transcendence to the Absolute. What we fail to understand is this: Why does one feel that he is alienated from the spirit? This leads to the theocentric concept of freedom which may be left undiscussed here.

3. Freedom and Phenomena

The antagonistic relation of freedom with phenomena is Kant's[73]. Kant's concept of freedom is "freedom from". Unless we are completely free from our bodily inclinations, from the phenomenal world, value attainment is never perfect. We want to be free from nomity; we aspire to be close to nomity. Social values are all fallacious. The only jewel which shines by its own light (free from phenomenal darkness) is the jewel of "good will".

Freedom being a property of transcendental self which can never be made into an object of knowledge is postulated and not provable. Freedom is not a proposition, it is a supposition. Thought, in its reflective moment, discovers the moral rule or the Categorical Imperative. Moral law is criteriological—it is not so much a law as a rule of deciding what a law is. As Kant's ethics is concerned mainly with the prescription, injunctions or rules of moral actions, we may call it Deontic or rule-ethics.

Man is essentially transcendental and only incidentally embodied, if existence be no hindrance to the essence then ability would have no situational or contextual limit—it would not be bound by space or time or even death. Kant realized that *a priorism* practiced in an immodest form will produce a negative effect. He favours modest *a priorism*. Both in pure reason and practical reason, matter is dummy, form is predominant. So far as pure reason is concerned, Kant made sensibility the correlate of form, but it was a dummy. So far as practical reason is concerned, Kant declared that only the Categorical Imperative has a form-day-to-day moral injunctions or material maxims are blind matter. Synthetic components of ethical judgments are dummy partners. Otherwise, we have rationalistic or conditional ethics. But conditional morality is no morality at all. Hence, the criterion of morality must be universal (denial of which is impossible and which is everywhere applicable). And its universality demands that it will be free of will-content or objective reference. Kant believed in the absolute freedom of all finite beings but this cannot be achieved if the world is not rational. So, Kant admitted the presence of a teleological unity between the material world and spiritual world. In the third critique, Kant draws the idea of harmony from the idea of God. That man belongs to the sensible order or sphere is evident. And as such, he is subject to the laws of determined causality. But his moral life manifests his freedom, and as free, he belongs to the noumenal order or sphere. Man, a being in the sensible (causal) world, is at the same time a being which possesses a property, viz., freedom. Though the idea of this property remains outside of the causal principles, yet this property belongs to man. And to be free is to be a spirit. There is, thus, a being above the world, namely the *spirit* of man. Furthermore, to be free in virtue of a spiritual principle is to be a person. The living corporeal being is besouled (animal). If it is a person, it is a human being.

Does this mean that man is split, as it were, into two elements? It obviously means that we can distinguish between man as noumenon and man as phenomenon. But though man possesses this dual nature, there is a unity of consciousness. This unity is manifested in moral consciousness. Man's freedom can translate itself into action within the world. There is, in man, an active but supersensible principle which, independent of Nature and of Natural causality, determines phenomena and is called freedom. As for Kant personality is de-historic, he makes little room for the perceptual subtleties, discriminating abilities made by the agent in a given situation. The situation in which an agent acts is never presented to the subject as an objective determination-situation is always a situation for a subject—it is coloured by his ideas, prejudices, biases and value-commitments. Conformity to a fixed moral rule, which is situation and condition—invariant, is sterile. Kant said that "ought" depends on "ability"; we shall supplement Kant by saying that "ability" depends on existence. In a particular situation, man's ability to choose is an expression of his value schedule which, again, is influenced by his

particular form of life. The denial of context—neutral value content—
does not necessarily imply acceptance of an extreme sort of scepticism.
Values possess relative autonomy only; they are only partly context—
neutral but not wholly context—invariant. This is so because human
beings do not enjoy absolute freedom as Kant imagined them to enjoy.
Freedom for man is not absolute because being detached from everything
around him, (his own intentions and motivations), he cannot take a
decision. Thus, finite man enjoys situational freedom, i.e. freedom as
encountered by finite beings *in* their situations. Kant said that in order
to be free, the self must be supremely subject. Phenomena-encountering,
object-constituting self is not free; we shall insist that it is the very nature
of the self to be world-encountering. The self which takes a decision is
a self-encountering-the-other and this "other" includes among other
things the objectified "I". To recognize the necessity of encountering
the obstacles and to try to overcome them as a result of which the
obstacles are melted and dissolved, and last but not the least, to be engaged
in the attempt to overcome the road—blocks is to be moral, to be free.

Kant could talk of absolute freedom because he had in his mind the
concept of pure individual consciousness—the pure ego to which he
accorded a purely formal ("analytic") unity. Following Strawson,[74] we
may say that "Pure ego" as a primary concept cannot exist—the primitive
concept is the concept of a person which is the concept of a type of entity
such that *both* predicates ascribing states of consciousness and predicates
ascribing corporeal characteristics are equally applicable to a single
individual of that single type. We raise two important questions which
are not independent of one another, viz., (1) why are states of consciousness
ascribed to anything at all? and (2) Why are they ascribed to the very
same thing as certain corporeal characteristics, a certain physical situation,
etc.? Our answer is that a necessary condition of states of consciousness
being ascribed at all is that they should be ascribed to the *very same thing*
as certain corporeal characteristics, a certain physical situation, etc. It
means that the states of consciousness can be ascribed only to persons.
Is the concept of person, then, a sort of compound of two kinds of subjects
a subject of experiences (pure ego) and a subject of corporeal attributes?
No, for it becomes impossible to show how we could come by the idea
of different, distinguishable identifiable subjects of experiences, *if this
idea is thought of as logically primitive*, as a logical ingredient of a person,

the latter being composed of two subjects. For there could never be any question of assigning an experience as such, to any subject other than one itself; and therefore never any question of ascribing it to a subject at all. Hence, "pure ego" cannot exist as a primitive concept; it can exist only as a secondary, non-primitive concept which requires explanation in terms of the primitive concept of a person. Also, with the demolition of pure ego, its autonomous free will is demolished.

The problem concerning freedom (as power to decide) and phenomena is often formulated as a conflict between freedom and determinism. The reasons presupposing such a conflict are as follows: (1) If determinism is true, man cannot be ethically responsible and since freedom of decision implies responsibility, it follows that if determinism is true, we do not have freedom of decision.

(2) If determinism is true, then man cannot be an active agent and since freedom of decision implies that man is an active agent, it follows that we have no freedom of decision.

(3) If determinism is true, then we do not have it in our power to decide otherwise than the manner in which we, in fact, did.

Of these, (3) is the most important and can explain the meaning of others. Still, (3) appears to be obscure. It requires clarification. There are three senses of the expression that a person's decision could not have been different. They are as follows:

(1) The decision was connected to other factors by relations which are valid for 100 per cent of such decision of which it is an instance.
(2) The decision is explainable on the basis of a well-confirmed hypothetic-deductive system, its observables are of inter-subjective power and its general hypothesis is universal.
(3) The decision was related to other factors by well-confirmed statistical relations.

The question which is relevant to our present concern is this: Do any of these senses imply that there is a sense in which a person did not have it in his power to decide otherwise, in any of these senses of "having a decision in one's power"? Does the statement that a person's decision D, in the situation S, is explainable on the basis of a well-confirmed hypothetico-deductive system? Perhaps not. The arguments which are intended to show that human decisions are explainable on the basis of a well-confirmed hypothesis are full of confusions. Human behaviour is not amenable to strict laws. Each individual is unique and not exactly like anyone else. Even if there is an order in the phenomena of human actions, it is to so complex as to elude discovery permanently. Thus, the above arguments prove that a man's decision may be connected with other factors but this connection need not be causal. This means that none of the senses can prove that causality implies powerlessness. It is true that if by the word "Power" we mean a transempirical frame of reference, then there may be a conflict between the causal principle and our power to decide. Man's power to decide is not the something which we have either in full or not at all. It is a matter of degree and individual variation what one man can do is not necessarily what another man can. What we can do in one situation may be different from what we can in another. The degree of power is determined by the character, conception and a number of factors. The sense in which it is important that the person could have decided otherwise does not directly have anything to do with whether his decision was uncaused. Still, there remains a problem. If a person's decisions has nothing to do with what is causally determined, then how can there be the way of resolving this dichotomy? Let us see.

4. Freedom in Decision and Causality in Prediction: Tested

A satisfactory explanation of the concept of a man's freedom in decision requires an adequate understanding of the role of human body in thought and action. It is in and by his body a person can be free and think objectively, i.e. intend objects. It is again in and by his body that a person can draw a significant line of demarcation between a natural phenomenon and a mental one ("this hand raises" and "I raise my hand"). To think is to act in a certain way (towards an object). To act is to attempt to achieve a certain goal. Choice involves thought. It is also under the influence of thought that we decide. Given certain possible ends, it makes sense to say "I have decided to choose this end and not that." It was possible for us to decide otherwise than we have, in fact, "decided". And the possibilities of decision are *influenced* by the thought of certain factors, viz., (1) whether an intended end can be realized in a given situation; (2) if it can be realized by what alternative means and with what probabilities; (3) what side effects and after-effects the choice of a given means may have apart from probably yielding the intended ends are jointly realizable or not. Many decisions are influenced by factual and valuational consideration. Given a fact, context or situation to decide this way rather than that also makes sense. In either case, the context is not completely *given*; it is partly given and partly *constructed*. But, for both production and consumption of cause, we must have a body. Decision is not a kind of bodily behaviour; but to decide we need a body. It is a condition of decision. Perhaps, in disembodied God, decision takes place "naturally", while in human cases, it is always influenced by so many contingencies such as expectation, information, valuation, etc. To accept this as a logic of decision is to state that in an act of decision, a person cannot be free from bodily considerations.

Causalism is the doctrine which states that all natural events have causes and since the only evidence we can have for belief in the validity of causal doctrine is empirical; i.e., the success of our predictions, so its denial is not self-contradictory. Predictability and determinism are not interchangeable terms although the two are related. Unpredictability does not entail indeterminism, because it is compatible with the existence of a theoretically determined system of such vast complexity that it is beyond human power to make correct predictions. Determinism is the doctrine which states that every event must have a causal ancestor and there cannot be any causal progenitors. Broad has offered this sort of analysis as well[75]. It means that if P is the total cause of R and Q is the total cause of P, then we call both P and Q the "causal ancestors"of R. If, in such a series there is a stage in which a term contains a cause factor that it is not completely determined, then the series will end there. Such a term is called the "causal progenitor" of such a series. We can definitely reject indeterminism if it asserts that nothing is determined, because we know something are indetermined; but if it asserts merely that not everything is determined it cannot be rejected offhand. The only evidence we can have for the belief that a state of affairs is determined is measured by the degree by which we can control, predict, construct, etc. If it be the rational explanation of causal determinism, then it cannot rule out the possibility of the power of following an alternative coures of actions. But how?

The issue with which we shall engage ourselves next is this: is freedom of decision compatible with the notion of causal determination? If it be so, wherein lies their compatibility, in the field of natural events or in the realm of human actions or in persons?

As to the first alternative, it can be said that since natural events do not possess any consciousness, the viewpoint there is no question of their making free decisions. Some thinkers hold that pure matter is not completely inert and that there is spontaneity in it. But such a view goes against our apprehension and experience. So far as our experience goes, natural events are subject to causal determination. Hence, causality cannot be shown to be compatible with freedom in the domain of natural phenomena. Concerning the second alternative, we may say that human actions are necessarily free, though this freedom has certain limits. So, causality cannot be shown to be compatible with man's capacity to decide freely in case of human actions.

Now we shall raise the following question: Is causality compatible with freedom in the case of a "person", in Strawson's sense? A person—thinks Strawson—is a single particular to which we can ascribe not only "M-predicates" (material-object-predicates) but also "P-predicates" (person-predicates); persons are with things in a spatio-temporal framework and distinguishable from other things, in virtue of the fact that P-predicates which are not applicable to other things are applicable to persons. Thus, both bodily behaviours and mental acts are constituents of personal identity. The decision, which a person takes, is certainly not a form of bodily behaviour, but body is a condition of decision. The embodied self is placed in a concrete situation (partly given and partly constructed) in which he is to exercize his freedom, to take his decision. But as an embodied self, a person belongs to a causal world and is subject to causal laws. But his subjection to causal laws is not a strict one since his reflective awareness brings in a transformation and modification in his constructive knowledge of the operations of the laws of nature. Again, as a person belongs to the world of values and can push the constraint he faces little beyond and his power to do so is *relatively* determined by his strength, ability, chosen-values, etc., he is relatively free. Let us try to frame the conditions of a person's being free which are in conformity with the conditions of person's being caused.

(1) Personal freedom is a sort of phenomenon not to be exhausted by causal analysis.

(2) It is an ability to be aware of and pursue to the alternative courses of action.

(3) It is the freedom enjoyed by situational, temporal, finite beings.

(4) Person's freedom involves an element of spontaneity or activity.

While sharing Strawson viewpoint that there are continuing personal identities in the world which can be identified and reidentified, we are unwilling to admit that the conceptual framework under which the person acts is unchangeable or fixed. What knowledge we may possess, we can always step back from that knowledge and ask ourselves: "How, in the light of that knowledge, shall I decide to ask?" This possibility of stepping back, this recessiveness of the "I", no increase in our scientific knowledge could possibly destroy and this "recessiveness of the 'I' constitutes freedom. A deterministic theory leaves no room for the fundamental distinction between a man's explaining to us, in terms of norms, why he has certain desires, certain intentions, certain attitudes, and some other person's explanation in terms of causes, why he has those particular desires, intentions and attitudes. At least, this is true for any form of determinism "which entails that the common-place scheme of explanation of conduct be replaced by a neutral vocabulary of natural law". Finally, as in a personal consciousness, we have shown that causality is continuous with human freedom, so it would not be unfair to say that the antagonistic relation between causality and a man's power to decide otherwise rests ultimately upon a serious confusion.

CHAPTER VI

The Logic of Causal Discourse

In this chapter, I shall re-examine my position with reference to the problem of the logic of causal discourse. My main line of argument is designed to assess the answers to the following three questions:

(1) What makes a proposition causal?
(2) What makes an inference causal?
(3) Can causal propositions be adequately translated into an extensional language?

I would argue to show (3a) that the implication of a causal law is different both from material implication and strict implication. In this connection, I will refer to the concerned views which have evoked considerable interest in recent times. I shall examine the logic of causal proposition only to the extent it is relevant to the development of my main arguments. In the concluding section of the chapter, I propose to round off my arguments highlighting two points. Firstly, is there any unity or discontinuity between the enquiries of causal and non-causal, e.g. normative discourses? Secondly, is there any rational way of explaining the relation? My main interest lies in arguing for a theory of explanation that is more or less common to causal as well as non-causal enquiries.

1. What Makes a Proposition Causal?

The logic of causal discourse seeks to develop a language to express causal propositions which are more precise and explicit than those expressible in the language of everyday discourse. Let us take an example of the ordinary inductive formulation of a particular causal proposition: the striking of a matchstick against matchbox causes fire. The question is:

what do we mean by the word "cause"? Ordinarily, by *cause*, we mean something which produces or brings about something. But what does "produce" mean? If it means the same as "cause", then we are back to the same problem from where we started. The point is the identification of the characters which a cause must have in order to give rise to an effect. It is taken for granted that the statements which can be verified by direct observation are empirical statements. But, do we observe that one event *causes* another? If we do so, then what is it that we observe when the effect is produced? It is true that we observe someone scratching a match with a stick and see a flame. But, what precisely do we observe that scratching the match causes the match to light? To say that C causes E is not merely to say that C precedes E, for many events occur without causing them. It is evident that we actually are in possession of some kind of criterion which enables us to distinguish between events that merely follow each other and events that cause each other. But how can we verify that the taking of some medicine is not only the antecedent but also the cause of the recovery of the patient? In this connection, I refer to the views of Schlick[76] who regards that there seems to be two different ways of such verification.

(1) If, by the application of medicine many times and perhaps on different patients, we find that in every single case a person suffering from a particular disease is cured, we should say that the use of the medicine was not a mere chance, but was caused by it. It means that if C is regularly followed by E, then C is the cause of E. Therefore, the observation of the regularity constitutes a sufficient reason for speaking of cause and effect. Against this view which identifies causality with regularity, it can be argued that nothing is more regular than the succession of day and night. It is universally accepted that we do not call the one cause and the other effect. Since the verification theory tells us that the meaning of a proposition lies in the method of its verification, it is meaningful only in so far as it is verifiable. Hence, the real difficulty arises: how many times should we observe the causal "nexus" or connection? No number will be considered satisfactory. The proposition "C is the cause of E" seems to mean nothing but that "C" is always followed by "E", but this latter proposition can, unfortunately, never be verified on account of the "always" it contains. Verification is possible if and only if, a finite number is substituted for "always" and no finite number is

satisfactory for it does not exclude the possibility of exceptions. Further, if the verification is never considered as complete and final, then we shall have to admit that we simply have no clear concept of causality. This aspect of Schlick's argument is not unreasonable. The problem may be made clearer by considering another alternative, i.e. does the cause occur after the effect? Supposing that I have in mind a goal that I want to attain, will this cause me to do certain things in the present? If we reflect even briefly on this matter, we shall see that it is not really the future event that does the causing. The future event has not yet occurred and is not yet there to do causing. What causes us to behave in a certain way in the present is the vision or thought of the goal itself which does not "exist" now. Can we be quite sure that no instance will ever occur of a cause that follows its effect rather than precedes it? Most probably, everyone would be willing to say that the characteristic of not occurring after the effect is one of the defining characteristics of a cause. We can never speak of a rain falling today as reviving the crops yesterday. So, a cause never occurs after its effect. The use of the word "cause" is such that if one event is said to be the cause of another, it is implied that the latter precedes or, at any rate, does not succeed the event which is said to be the effect. In this connection, Ayer argues[77] that it is very difficult to understand why one should insist on making it impossible for a later event to cause an earlier one. He holds that there are many to whom the very idea of a later event causing an earlier would seem an absurdity—not because it does violence to ordinary usage, but because they cannot conceive how something which does not yet exist could already be exerting its influence. On this assumption, a thing which already exists can bring into being something which had not existed hitherto. But it is a mere psychological appeal, as Ayer looks at it. For, to say that A is the cause of B is to say that either A is a sufficient condition of B or that it is both a sufficient and a necessary condition. If we interpret the situation in terms of a later event and of an earlier event, we find that if an earlier event is a necessary condition of a later one, the later event is a sufficient condition of the earlier and if an earlier event is a sufficient condition of the later, the later is a necessary condition of the earlier. Also, if either one is a necessary and sufficient condition of the other, then an earlier event is both a necessary and sufficient condition of a later event, the later event is, in turn, both a necessary and sufficient condition of the earlier one, i.e. to say the relation is reciprocal. To quote Ayer: "If for example, it is a necessary condition of my suffering from malaria that I should have been bitten by an anopheles mosquito, then my suffering from malaria is a sufficient condition of my having previously bitten. If my taking arsenic in the appropriate quantities is a sufficient condition of my subsequently dying in a certain way, then my dying in that certain way is a necessary condition of my previously taking the arsenic. I shall not be taking the arsenic unless I were about to die, just as I should not be suffering from malaria unless I had been bitten by a mosquito. And if let us say it is in certain circumstances both a necessary and sufficient condition for a projectile to rebound at a given angle and with a given velocity from a wall, that it should have struck the wall from such and such angle with such and such a velocity then to rebounding in that way from the wall is also a necessary and sufficient condition of its striking it. It would not have rebounded in that way unless it had so struck it, but equally, it would not have struck it in that way unless it had been going to rebound." [78]

Apart from the above stipulation, there is no sufficient ground for believing that a cause cannot succeed its effect. So, why should we make this stipulation? Ayer suggests that we may seem to have just as much reason for believing that earlier events are caused by later events as far believing that the earlier events cause the later events. But this suggestion is not to be regarded as reasonable. It is true that the cause constitutes both a necessary and a sufficient condition for the occurrence of the effect. But mere necessity and sufficiency of a condition cannot account for the causal relation as a one-way direction. To this, the notion of productivity should be added, and Ayer—true to his empiricist persuasion—does not care for the acceptance of such a principle which, even in his liberal and revised sense, is not verifiable. That is why, the causal relation is so construed that the passage of the spark through the mixture of gases is the cause of their transformation into water, but the formation of the water is not the cause of the passage of the spark. Since a cause cannot succeed its effect, so the question of the verification of this succession does not arise. Similarly, we have seen that a cause is not any event that occurs before another event.

Let us now continue to study the other way of the verification of a causal proposition. Suppose there is a case in which we believe that we should have to wait for any repetition of sequence treatment recovery in order to assert a causal relation between two events. So, there must be a second way of verifying a causal statement independent of the observation of regularity. Those who believe in this second way will immediately add that it is the only real way. The traditional metaphysical view on this understanding is that there is some kind of necessary connection between "C" and "E" when "C" causes "E". It is not enough to say that E follows C in a certain way but that C must be followed by E. The only sense that we can attach to this idea is purely logical. Since the understanding of a causal relation is not a process of logical reasoning, Schlick would not accept this alternative. What is called causal necessity is altogether different from logical necessity. Schlick's line of argument is as follows: we learn that the causal relation between two separate events is actually explained when we conceive the two as being connected by a chain of intermediate events. But if we look for the causal link connecting two events together, we cannot find anything but another event. Whatever can be observed and shown in the causal chain will be the links but it would be nonsensical to look for the linkage. This shows that we are perfectly wrong when we think that this chain could consist of anything but events and that it could be a kind of mysterious tie called "causality". That the idea of such a "tie" is due to a faulty process of thinking has been shown by Hume. Sometimes, it has been thought that what Hume says is true enough of events in an external world but there are some events in which we are aware of a necessary connection, viz., those involving our own will. But Hume tries to show that in some cases the event does not follow upon the volition, so there can be no necessary connection between the volition and the event. Thus, the causal proposition cannot express the relation of logical entailment between the cause and its effect. We agree with Schlick in holding that Hume's analysis is right in so far as the empirical verification of the necessary connection involving natural events as well as our own will are concerned. But the point which is more fundamental may be stated thus: if the test of the truth of a statement constitutes its significance then the causal statement of the form "E", because of "C" cannot be made significant. But it is unreasonable to think that the whole of the meaning content of a statement is exhausted by its verifiable content. If there is a surplus of meaning extent of statement that is not exhausted by its verifiable content, then the assumption that verification constitutes the genuine criterion for the meaningfulness of a statement is groundless. Therefore, we should not accept this analysis of ordinary inductive formulation of a particular causal proposition.

Let us note the general features of any formulation of a causal statement. In this connection, we may perhaps profitably look into the view of Mario Bunge,[79] who observes this problem in the light of the nature of a causal principle. This interpretation appears to be true to us. Bunge opines that the correct formulation of the causal principle seems to be of the following form:

(1) C, therefore E or,
(2) E, because of C.

Both these statements assert a bond between C and E and also assert the existence of both, but an adequate formulation of the causal principle should not involve the assumption that "C actually exists" but should say that if C is the case, then E will be the case. In short, the statement must be conditional. The formulation then becomes: If C, then E and in this expression "C" and "E" may be taken to designate particulars belonging to classes of concrete objects, and so on. Logically, "C" and "E" may be regarded either as individual or as propositional variables. In the former case (2) is an incomplete expression, whereas in the latter case it is just a compound proposition. It may be convenient to regard "C" and "E" as kinds of free variables. But then, in order to obtain from (2) a proposition, we have to specify the range of the terms involved, i.e. we have to affix a quantifier to (2) and this will now be done.

As to the first formulation of the causal principle stating relations among variables "C" and "E" symbolizing kinds of facts or rather definite features of facts, there might be the following possibilities: that it holds *sometimes*, or that it holds *always*, i.e. for all values of the variables. Since causal relation is supposed to universally hold the first formulation is incorrect. Without exception, repetition may be added to this formulation, i.e. E, whenever C is the case. The result becomes (3) If C, E always or,

(3)[1] For all C and E, if C is the case then E is also the case.

The notions that are usually associated with the idea of causality, viz., conditionalness, existential succession, constancy and all these are applicable to this formulation. Conditionalness is not only peculiar to causal lawfulness; it is a demand which must be satisfied by any kind of law statement. Existential succession means that the cause is existentially prior to its effect. The word "constancy" designs to indicate the fact that if cause is the case, effect will ensue invariably. This is what the all-operator always means. The formulation (3) of the causal principle asserts that the causal bond is *conditional, unsymmetrical* and *necessary*. Are these characters sufficient to describe causation unambiguously? The first and the most fundamental objection that can be raised against this formulation is that it neglects the uniqueness of the causal bond. It is not possible to say that there is one-to-one correspondence between "C" and "E". C may denote any one of the sufficient conditions or causes which make room for multiple causation. Uniqueness is a characteristic trait of causation and it is altogether absent when there are many-to-one connections between causes and its effects. If only necessary and sufficient conditions are taken into account as antecedents in a causal connection, i.e. if simple causation is meant then the formulation (3) must be reformulated into (4) "if C then (and only then) E always". The statement lastly formulated is a universal conditional statement expressing the constant conjunction of two terms and it does not state a genetic connection between the two but an invariable coincidence. But the constant conjunction view of causation is hardly defensible. The Humean formula of causation, i.e. constant conjunction view of connection neither accounts for the uniqueness nor for the genetic character of the relation between "C" and "E". A law of correlation is not a causal law. It can never be said that a given entity is produced by another entity; rather, the two are regularly associated. Since the element of productivity is absent in their correlation, the relation cannot be considered as causal.

Now, what is common to both ordinary and scientific usage of the word that causation far more than a category of relation is a category of genetic connection, i.e. a way of producing things out of other things. This efficacy of the efficient cause is what we can express in a third approximation,

(5) If C happens then (and only then) E is always produced by it. This formulation goes beyond a mere constant conjunction of events. It asserts that the effect is not merely conjoined with the cause, but is engendered by it. The characters that are assigned here: (a) conditionalness; (b) uniqueness; (c) one-sided dependence of the effect upon the cause, invariability of the connection; and (d) productivity. The statement "If

C happens then (and only then) E is always produced by it" is an adequate formulation of the causal principle. If we want to further refine the statement of the necessary-production formulation of causation, we find:

If C happens under the same conditions then (and only then) E is always produced by it (6). It asserts that other things being equal, the same cause always produces the same effect. But is (6) really better than (5)? In order to answer this question, we must distinguish two cases, viz., the "conditions" and the "cause". If the conditions are connected with C—if together with C they constitute a single causal complex C—then the cause cannot be called simple but complex, e.g. "if a match is struck, it lights". At least the following conditions must be assumed for the link to hold, viz., the match should be dry and there must be enough oxygen. We can reconstruct the above statement by saying that if a dry match is struck in an oxygen-containing atmosphere, the match lights. In short, if the conditions are linked to the cause, C may be taken as the chief cause (necessary but not sufficient). The conditions being the subsidiary causes, it is the whole complex of determinants which constitute necessary and sufficient cause of its effect. The viewpoint that the relation between a cause and its conditions is an essential relation that has been defended, among others, by Mill and the Naiyāyikas of India. Mill regards that in every causal situation, it is very natural to single out one of the antecedents under the denomination of *cause*, calling the other *conditions*. But this attempt is pointless. Mill says:

"The real cause then, philosophically speaking, is the sum total of the conditions, positive and negative taken together; the whole of the contingencies of every description, which, being realized, the consequent invariably follows"[80].

So, the distinction between cause and condition is often arbitrarily drawn, and in that case corresponds to no fundamental distinction. This means that the conditions and the cause are interdependent. From the Nyāya standpoint the cause must be a complex group—a collocation of all causal antecedents (sāmagri)[81] and it is in Mill's language, "the sum total of all the conditions, positive and the negative taken together". The necessary and sufficient characters of a cause are completely dependent upon the fulfilment of other preconditions. That is to say, the genuine causes must be the group of causes or conditions. It is true that there is an important difference between Mill's analysis of the relation of cause and effect and the Nyāya analysis of the cause-effect relation. For Mill, in a causal situation, a cause is sufficient for the occurrence of a thing, whereas the Naiyāyikas holds that in a causal situation, a cause is both a necessary and sufficient condition for the occurrence of a thing. In spite of all these differences of opinion, what is evident and interesting for us to note here is that the connection of a cause and its conditions is an intrinsic one and maintained by both Mill and the Nyāya School. Also, we agree with this aspect of their analysis.

Thus, turning now to the original question, it can be said that if the conditions are linked to the cause, the formulation (6) can be reduced to the formulation (5) and then, the formulation (5) becomes "It is the whole complex of determinants which constitute the necessary and sufficient cause of its effect". If the accompanying conditions are contingent upon the cause, then the cause cannot be regarded as the necessary and sufficient producer of the effect. Thus, the formulation (6) cannot be regarded as a better formulation of the causal principle. It would be better to retain the necessary production formulation as a faithful schematic representation of causal relation. Consequently, a proposition is causal if and only if it is the substitution instance of the formula "If C then (and only then) E is always (in most cases) produced by it". Cautious scientists might object to the "productivity" in this formulation of the causal proposition and the charge levelled against our formulation may be met by stating that the content of a causal proposition should not be exhausted with its *empirical* content and "productivity" constitutes the essential *unempirical* content of a causal proposition.

2. What Makes an Inference Causal?

In an inference ordinarily, we pass from the facts known to the facts unknown. Also, whether an inference would be causal or not would depend exclusively upon the nature of its major premise. What is the relation between two kinds of state of affairs of a premise, A and B, which we have in mind when we speak of them as causally connected? These answers are, respectively: (a) "The relation consists in a constant conjunction of A with B"; and (b) "The relation is a logical relation of entailment between A and B". Needless to say, once these straight forward answers have been given, each is immediately surrounded with a host of qualifications and classifications designed to counter the standard objections from the opposite camp.

Let us closely look into an empiricist's answer. An empiricist holds that to say "C causes E" means simply that C is a set of conditions such that whenever they are fulfilled. E happens and whenever E happens they have all been fulfilled. Causality, here, not involve any connection between cause and effect except the connection of regular sequence. The effect always or usually follows the cause; the cause does not in any reasonable sense of the term makes a difference to, or produce, the effect, but is simply constantly followed by it. If the regularity thesis be the final answers to the question, then the major premises of a causal inference must be the proposition that expresses the mere assemblage of intrinsically unconnected facts. This view of causal generalization has been rejected by many thinkers, for the theory of regular sequence presents causality in a manner altogether different from what we mean by causality. Ordinarily, it characterizes that: (1) the effect is held to be continuous with and dependent on something in the cause on account of which the two are intrinsically connected with each other; (2) the demand for causes is primarily the demand for reasons and that implies that there is a logical connection between the two; (3) the cause is held to produce the effect actively; and (4) the necessity involved in a causal relation. It should be clarified that here we are not suggesting that the ordinary view of causation, which we have just mentioned, is clear and unambiguous. We are merely insisting on the point that the ordinary view of causation differs rightly or wrongly from the theory of regular sequence. On the regularity view, the only objective relation left between cause and effect is that of regular temporal sequence. There are thinkers who believe that an account of causality includes—besides propositions asserting this objective relation—propositions of a psychological character. Both Ramsey and Braithwaite share this belief. For Ramsey, causality is regularity together with an attitude of expectation for the future, but this psychological proposition does not reveal the objective relation between cause and effect. Further, the fact that everyone believes that an objective relation of regular sequence does hold between the events P and Q is left unnoticed for all practical purposes. The only objective relation that draws our attention is the relation of regular temporal sequence. This type of analysis amounts to the denial of any specific relation of causation. It is a relation in which relates many causally unrelated events.

The argument in favour of the regularity theory may fall under two heads: (1) the difficulties involved in other views of causation may be a sufficient reason for advocating the regularity theory; and (2) the regularity view is best vouchsafed by empirical evidence. Since the fact that we could not give a satisfactory statement of what else there was in causality would not prove that there was nothing else beyond regularity, so the main attraction of the regularity theory lies in the fact that regularity is indisputably given in experience. Here arises a dilemma. Either the advocates of the regularity theory should maintain that any event which occurs once will occur again, provided the relevant conditions are same. This is to state the principle of the uniformity of nature in a different way. Or, the advocates of the regularity theory should interpret the principle as simply covering only the observed regularities of the past. If this be the case, then "C is the cause of E" would signify only this much that "C has in all observed cases been regularly followed by E". To defend induction, we must appeal to some other principle which serves as to pass beyond the observed.

A novel attempt has been made by Ramsey[82] to escape between the horns of the dilemma. Induction may be made "reasonable" in the sense that it is a *useful* habit to form a kind of belief on the strength of past experience. But does this attempt really escape this dilemma? Answering it, one may argue that "reasonable" is used to mean the outcome of a useful habit, and the word "useful" means leading to opinions which are mostly true. It may be proved empirically that the habit of believing in inductive evidence has been useful in the past. But the habits which are useful in the past in producing true opinions will also be useful in the future, is obviously the result of another induction. This type of induction which serves as the ground of all other inductions cannot be called "reasonable" merely because in the sense of being useful, if any conclusion is said to be "reasonable" in the sense of being useful, one inductive conclusion that it will continue to be so, must itself be reasonable in a sense *other than* useful. Thus, the rationality of inductive arguments is not always explicable in terms of its usefulness. This point has been emphasized, among others, by Ewing [83].

In order to disprove the theory of regular sequence, we may turn now to the positive arguments that can be raised against the theory of regular sequence. (1) If scientific arguments are to have any validity at all, it must be possible in causal inference to argue legitimately from a set of conditions as a premise to an event as conclusion, but no inference can possibly be legitimate unless the premises really entail the conclusion. If science is to have any claim of truth, the cause must really necessitate the effect which is certainly something more that mere regular sequence. The relation of entailment in causation is perhaps very different in kind from that which justifies *a priori* inference in pure mathematics and logic. But any justification of induction becomes impossible if some sort of entailment relation is totally absent between a premise and its conclusion in an inference. (2) This argument is dependent on the notion of probability. If the regularity view is accepted as true, then all generalizations would be sheer coincidences. When there is a connection between the properties of C and E so that one really involves and does not just precede the other, then the coincidence is indeed removed. This is so because there is always a reason why E should always follow C, but not otherwise. The theory of regular sequence pretends not to go and yet it does go beyond the boundary of empirical evidence. Consequently, it fails to offer a cogent explanation of the nature of causal relation, which involves, among other things, uniform sequence.

Coming now to the other answer of the problem, we realize that the major premise of a causal inference expresses the relation of logical entailment between the two kinds of events. The argument of those who maintain that causal propositions express relations of logical entailment is of the same order as that which is used to support that causal inferences are often reasonable. They think that causal inferences are deductive inferences from ground to consequent. This analysis of causal inference has been seriously criticized by Ayer. His line of reasoning is as follows:

(1) No room of inductive inference is ever "reasonable" in the sense of being formally demonstrative. Demand for the justification of causal inference is unreasonable in the sense that it involves the application to inductive reasoning of a standard rationality that is applicable to deductive reasoning alone. The rationality of a causal inference is not demonstrative. Also, that which is not formally demonstrable is supported by strong inductive evidence. But from this, it does not follow that such inferences

can never be made reasonable in the sense in which this word is properly applicable to them. Ayer is right in thinking so.

(2) If there is a genuine difficulty about the justification of causal inference, the hypothesis of the active tendencies of material things would fail to fulfil the purpose for which it is designed. Granted, it is actually possible to observe a positive tendency to unbend in the bow. It cannot be demonstrated that the existence of the tendency is either a necessary or even a sufficient condition of the occurrence of the event, of which it is supposed to be a cause. For instance, we observe an event which we take to be of the nature P, and the evidence of past observations is that events of P kind have always, under similar conditions, been succeeded by events of the nature X. Let us now suppose that we are in doubt whether this gives us any reason at all for believing that events of P kind and X kind are universally conjoined or that they will be conjoined in a particular case in the future. One may point out the fact that our difficulty is imaginary on the grounds that the proposition that an instance of X will occur in these conditions is logically entailed by the proposition that the event we are observing is an instance of P. This point may be made clearer by the idealistic assumption that the function performed by the thing constitutes its essence. It means that as long as a thing is P, it must not act differently. But the trouble is that we must also be more doubtful whether this really is an instance of P, provided we already have reason to believe that every instance of P is not logically but factually conjoined under Q conditions with an instance of x. To this theory, Ayer comments that this is not the ordinary practice. Ayer's objection does depend upon the logic of practice and if only practical considerations are taken into account then very many relations of things of the world cannot be made intelligible. So, our inability to justify the thesis of logical entailment by means of practical test cannot be sufficient grounds for its rejection. The rejection of the major premise of causal inference as expressing the relation of logical entailment would be a genuine rejection only if we suppose that only sense experience or empirical verification constitutes the necessary and sufficient condition of a test of truth. The problem now is: what positive account can we give of the nature of the major premise of a causal reasoning? We may heartily accept the regularity theory as a partial explanation of the nature of a causal relation. That is

to say, we may grant that causality involves, among other things, uniform sequence. Further the argument from probability, which is a special form of the theory of regularity, can only be legitimately used to establish causal laws if we assume a view of causation according to which it is at least *closely analogous* to logical entailment. It is often said, however, that in a causal situation, the cause entails its effect means that the effect is contained in the cause or that the effect and its cause are identical. They are not two but one, just as in an inference the premise entails the conclusion means that the conclusion is contained in the premise or that the premise and its conclusion are at the bottom identical. These statements are preposterous in the context of a causal situation; the effect cannot be contained in the cause, for otherwise, it would not be a different event. The logical connection between a cause and its effect is not analytic but synthetic. The fact that we can and do always obtain new knowledge about reality through causal inference proves that causal relation is synthetic. That causal relation is in some respect the relation of logical entailment is confirmed by the fact that we can argue from the cause to the effect. It seems to imply that in some way, the one logically involves the other; otherwise could we infer the one from the other? If logical relations can only hold between propositions and not between facts in the real world and if all inferences are merely analytic which have nothing to do with the realities to which the symbols refer, then it would be impossible to suppose that a logical connection between cause and effect could ever be perceived by any mind. The rationalist philosophers are going too far when they identify cause with logical ground. The relation between a cause and its effect is in one respect analogous to—but is certainly not identical with—the relation subsisting between logical or mathematical propositions. On this interpretation, "to entail" does not mean "to include".

Secondly, the view that causal relation is at least closely analogous to that of logical entailment seems to be a necessary presupposition of induction. It is essential for induction to believe that what happened under certain conditions in the past is likely to happen under certain conditions in the future. But how could we possibly be justified in believing this? In the absence of any assumption of a necessary connection, the mere fact that B has followed A could give no grounds for expecting that it will do so on future occasions, and regular sequence of B on A would be an incredible coincidence.

Certain objections raised against the above view are to be answered now. First, it may be objected that since we must admit that we cannot find any necessary connection underlying natural laws, postulation of necessity can be of no help at least so far as physical causation is concerned. One may respond to this objection by stating that the passage from the observed to the unobserved can never be justified unless an "unseen" necessity is postulated to exist between what we regard as the cause and what we think of as the effect. We claim to have the justification to infer the effect from the cause and the cause from the effect. No inference can be valid unless the relation underlying it is like the relation of logical entailment which underlies a valid inference. Second, the probable character of a causal generalization has been subjected to a serious scrutiny. It is sometimes said that all inferences are either certain or fallacious. There is no intermediate turn to characterize an inference or argument. But if we had *a priori* insight into necessity—that the relation between A and B is a necessary relation—A would seem to be certainly true, but this we have not. If we cannot see whether there is a necessary connection between A and B, we cannot hope to prove it *a priori*; all that we can do is to find out whether A and B empirically go together in a sufficient number and relevant kind of circumstances and, in doing so, we can never be completely certain. Thirdly, it has been objected that the above attempt of defending causal inference reduces an inductive inference to a mere species of deduction. But why should it not be so? The old logical division of deduction and induction as two coordinate species of inference may not do justice to facts and it has never proved easy for logicians to maintain the distinction strictly. Also if induction is to be regarded as species of deduction, there are important differences which provide a justification for its separate treatment and distinguish it from all other kinds of deduction. For, unlike all other kinds of deduction, it depends on the assumption of a necessity which we do not see and this makes its conclusion always less certain than its premises, whereas in an ordinary deduction, such issues are equally certain. Even if there is a logical necessity in the physical world, it is not at all surprising that we would not be able to know anything of the "internal and immutable" nature of physical things and if so we cannot possibly expect to see what a physical event can or cannot entail. Further, we are never in a position to state the whole cause of an event but if causality involves entailment, then the whole cause (and not a part of it) will entail an event which will be the effect. Consequently, it must be admitted that causal entailment differs from all other cases of entailment because what is entailed here is not simultaneous with but succeeds what entails it.

From the above discussion, it follows that the causal character of an inference ultimately depends upon the causal nature of its hypothesis. Also, the causal character of a hypothesis is constituted by a kind of necessity whose empirical schema is a regular sequence, in accordance with which we can deductively draw the conclusion of an inference. In other words, the truth of a counter-evidence of a hypothesis is the sufficient condition of the falsification of the causal generalization. Since there is always a scope for the falsification of a causal generalization by means of empirical evidences, a causal inference cannot be completely identified with the deductive inference of the rationalists; rather the relation underlying every causal inference is closely *analogous* to the relation of logical entailment. We may characterize this relation as the relation of partial entailment. Partial entailment is not complete analalyticity; yet it is a necessity and not mere contingency. "Being Black" is not a necessary property of ravens; for the statement "this raven is not black", though false, is not contradictory. It would be logically false to deny this property in conjunction with the denial of the usual properties looked for in a thing called "raven". Though a single property can be denied without contradiction, the fact that it is in conjunction with others cannot be so denied. Such single properties are partially entailed properties. That is why, "the turning of a switch" partially entails the coming on of a light" and "the coming on of a light partially entails the turning of a switch". Thus, the necessity of a causal relation is to be attributed to the relation of partial entailment obtains between the things to be causally connected. A causal hypothesis is always *construed* or *conjectured* on the basis of the observation of general natural events.

3. Causal Propositions and Extensional Language

In this section, we shall be mainly concerned with the problem of translating causal propositions into an extensional language, for example, in the language of *Principia Mathematica*. It is obvious that conditional statements expressing causal connections are not intended as involving material implications. A. W. Burks, in his article "The logic of causal propositions" (*Mind*,1951), tried to exhibit the relation between causal propositions and other logical propositions. The implication involved in a causal law is different both from material and strict implication and Burks' calls it "causal implication". He has introduced the symbol "C" for it. Burks' system is distinguished by the use of a constant "C", signifying a relation of implication which holds between "p" and "q" when the conditions expressed by "p" are causally sufficient to make "q" true. The formulation "Ea C Da" asserts that the conditions expressed by "Ea" are causally sufficient to make "Da" true. But what is meant by sufficient conditions? Sufficient conditions are a set of conditions, complete with respect to negative properties as well as positive ones, sufficient to cause the state of affairs expressed by the consequent. A number of consequences follow if by "C" is meant "Causally sufficient".

The first consequence is that the argument from "Ea C Da" to "Da C Ea" is fallacious; so the statement C form "p C q .⊃. q C p" is fallacious.

The second consequence is that the antecedent of a causal implication may contain irrelevant conditions; on this interpretation, Ea C Da. ∴. Ea, Oa, .C.Da.

is a valid inference. The principle that governs this inference is p C q : ⊃ : pr. C. q.

If we strictly follow this principle, we can validly infer "Ea.~ Ea . C . Da" from the premise "Ea C Da". But ordinary usage goes against this inference.

The third consequence is that "C" expresses a transitive relation. p C q . q C r : ⊃ : p C r.

The acceptance of the leading principle allows us to predicate the relation of causal implication of events which are not contiguous in time and space. If we think that "C" connotes no temporal sequence, then a causal implication may be used to express causal relations of a non-temporal sort. As a result, transposition is valid: p C q . ⊃ . ~ q C ~ p; for if a cause is sufficient to produce an effect then the effect is a causally necessary condition of the cause and the absence of the effect causally implies the absence of the cause.

Due to these deviations, some of the arguments which are valid by means of the principle of causal propositions cannot be proved to be valid when expressed in ordinary languages. Ordinarily, we believe, for example, that the argument "If it rains he will wear his raincoat; therefore, if he does not wear his raincoat it would not rain" is invalid because rain could cause a person to wear a raincoat, but his wearing a raincoat has no causal influence on the weather.

The fourth consequence has to do with the validity of the principle of exportation. Supposing two conditions taken together are causally sufficient to produce an effect, it does not follow that if one condition is satisfied then the second is causally sufficient to produce the effect. So, the following statement—form is fallacious: $p\, q\,.\, C\,.\, r : \supset : p\, C\, q\,.\, C.\, r.$

Burks concludes that statements of ordinary usage involving causal implication must be construed as elliptical. An elliptical sentence is necessarily vague and it is impossible to decide its precise meaning with certainty. Finally, he regards that most assertions of causal implication are elliptical in this or in a similar manner.

Symbolic logicians have been able to interpret implications, i.e. statements of the form "If p then q" in an obvious and unconcealed departure from ordinary usage, as the meaning becomes "it is not the case that p and not q". In this way, they followed Russell who introduced the notion of material implication usually symbolized by "$\supset$", mainly because it was required by a truth functional theory of deductive inference. A deductive inference in the two valued propositional calculus is valid if the implication corresponding to it is a tautology, and whether or not it is a tautology is mechanically decidable by a truth table. It is obvious that conditional statements expressing causal connections are not intended as material implications. What, then, is the relation between causal implication (C) and material implication ($\supset$)? A very common use of a causal law is to make predictions following it, for example,

$(x)\ (Ex\ C\ Dx),\ Ea\ \therefore\ Da$
$(x)\ (Ex\ C\ Dx)\ \sim Da\ \therefore \sim Ea$

are valid arguments. The validity of these arguments shows that a causal implication implies its corresponding material implication, i.e. "$p\, C\, q\,.\,)\,.$ $p \supset q$" and "$(x)\ (Fx\ C\ Gx) \supset (x)\ (Fx \supset Gx)$".

Now the question is: do the converses of these relations hold? If they do so, then a causal implication must be equivalent to a material implication. As a result, the logic of causal propositions would reduce immediately to an extensional logic. But good arguments can be advanced to prove that the following equivalences are fallacious.

(1) $pCq \equiv p \supset q$
(2) $(x)(Fx \ C \ Gx) \equiv (x)(Fx \supset Gx)$ for "$p \supset q. \supset . pCq$"

and "$(x)(Fx \supset Gx) . \supset (x) (Fx \ C \ Gx)$" are false. If (1) were valid, a false proposition would imply any proposition whatsoever. The well-known paradoxes of material implication are: (1) a true proposition is implied by any proposition whatsoever. If we interpret these two assertions in the light of the casual implication, we find that a cause, if absent, entails any effect. If (2) were valid, one could hold that a causal universal implies its corresponding material universal but still something more is meant by a causal universal than a mere material universal. In order to prove that (2) is invalid, Burks points out some undesirable consequences which follow from the assumption of its validity. For instance, "All the raven in this country are black" is a universal proposition true by accident and we could naturally symbolize it by "$(x) (Rx \supset Bx)$" rather than by "$(x)(Rx \ C \ Bx)$". Since it is true by accident, its corresponding conjunction "$(x) (Rx \supset Bx).\sim(x) (Rx \ C \ Bx)$" is true. But if we grant that a causal universal is equivalent to its corresponding material universal, the quoted conjunction becomes impossible. It follows then that a causal implication implies a material universal but the same is not *vice versa*. So, causal implication cannot be identified with material implication.

Restoring the correspondence between the ordinary and the technical meanings of "implication", Lewis suggests the relation of a strict implication ($\dashv$) holds between any two propositions p and q where it is not possible that p and $\sim$ q both would be true. In other words, the relation of strict implication ($\dashv$) holds between p and q whenever q is uniquely deducible from p. So far as the relation between a strict and a causal implication is concerned, Burks thinks that a strict implication implies a causal implication but not vice-versa. For instance,

1. $p \dashv q$ ("$\dashv$" strict implication)
2. $\sim \Diamond (p. \sim q)$ ("$\Diamond$"—logically possible)
3. pCq (p is a causally sufficient condition for q)

Since (1) implies (2) and (2) implies (3), so (1) implies (3), i.e. $p \dashv q. \supset .pCq$. One consequence of this principle is that it introduces causal paradoxes from the so-called paradoxes of strict implication. Strict implication has not solved the paradoxes of its own. Because an impossible proposition strictly implies any proposition whatsoever, it is clear then that there are paradoxes of causal implication. Corresponding to the implications with logically impossible antecedents, there are implications with causally impossible antecedents and corresponding to the implications with logically necessary consequents there are implications with causally necessary consequents, i.e. true by virtue of a causal law. The paradoxes of causal implication may be stated thus: a causally impossible antecedent causally implies any consequent and a causally necessary consequent is causally implied by any antecedent. In order to state this principle, Burks uses the symbols for the concepts of causal possibility ("$\Diamond$") and causal necessity ("$\boxed{C}$") which corresponds to the concepts of logical possibility ("$\Diamond$") and logical necessity ("$\Box$"). Symbolically stated, the paradoxes are as follows: (1) $\sim \Diamond$ p . C . p C q,

(2) $\boxed{C}$ p . C . q C p.

The concept of causal possibility and causal necessity can be related to the concepts of causal implication; just as the concepts of logical possibility and logical necessity can be related to the concept of strict implication. That is to say,

$$\boxed{C} (p \supset q) \equiv pCq$$
$$\Diamond p \equiv \sim \boxed{C} \sim p.$$

The above analyses lead Burks to state that a causal implication is implied by the corresponding strict implication and a causal implication implies its corresponding material implication with a modal operator. This suggests that causal propositions have a certain modal character; they are empirical rather than rational.

Burks' explanation can account for the failure of the truth functional language to translate a causal proposition. But what we object to is this: to argue that a strict implication implies its causal implication is to establish the rationalistic tenet that every logically necessary statement is causally necessary. Also, to say that causal implication is appropriate to all types of bi-unique connections, whether involving a genetic relation or not—suggests that it does not account for what is peculiarly causal. The systems of strict and causal implication can be distinguished from the system of material implication in terms of what is called their *strength*.

It is true that the logical systems of strict and causal implications comes into being when the truth—logic of propositions is supplemented by new and undefined terms namely, "Ⅎ" and "C". Some may justify this procedure as new "intuitive motivation" but the meaning of "intuitive motivation", as Henderson thinks[84], is obscure. So, Henderson has questioned the claim of those who want a new modal operator—that of the causally necessary to do work for which strict necessity is too strong and truth-functions too weak. Apart from that, the avoidance of paradox has been obvious throughout the principal motive of Burks' system. Sometimes it has been argued that Burks need not have admitted paradoxes as a necessary element in a causal logic. But we do not know whether he had avoided the paradoxes of strict implication on the grounds that they do not arise in the context of causal logic. It is true that Burks is right in holding that implicative statements involving causal relations cannot be made identical with material implication. Thus, when we try to express causal relation in an extensional language, the relation loses much of its inner characters.

4. Causal Implication and its Logical Correlate

No satisfactory logical correlate of the causal connection seems to have been discovered so far. An adequate verbal formulation of the causal connection should precede every attempt to formalize causal proposition and it should be pointed out that what is required is not an extensional or formal relation, but the determination of a type of semantic connection among terms that are relevant to each other. The logical aspect of the causal problem is semantical rather than syntactical. In logic, we can distinguish three relations among propositions, viz., logical implication, implication and material implication. The first is taken after G.E. Moore to be the converse of the relation of deducibility; the second implication is taken to be the converse of the wider relation of inferribility. The third is a truth-functional relation. Among these three, we can roughly place causal proposition to the category of implication that hold between propositions expressing causal connection of events. There are thinkers who believe that of these three, the concept of material implication is wider than the other two, that of logical implication is narrower than the other two; and that of implication is narrower than the first but wider than the third. Of these three relations, it can be said that the first is the weakest and the third is the strongest while the second is stronger than the first but weaker than the third.

The above division of the relations among propositions can be justified in the following manner. The conjunctive definition of material implication makes it clear that to say that a proposition materially implies another is to say that it is not the case that the first proposition is true while the second is false. And it is now easier to see what relations material implication stand to implication and logical implication. When it is said "p implies q", it is meant that q is inferrible from p. But if q is inferrible from p, then it is not the case that p is true and q is false. And this further means that whenever a proposition implies the other, it *also* materially implies the same. But the converse of this relation is not true. That is to say, a proposition may materially imply another proposition without implying it. In this sense, the concept of material implication is wider than that of implication. In comparing material implication with logical implication, we find the same thing when it is said that p logically implies q, it is said that it is impossible that p is true and q is false. And if it is impossible that p is true and q is false, then it is false that p is true and q is false, because modal logic states that if a proposition is impossible then it is also false. This proves that if a proposition logically implies another it also materially implies that other. This is the sense in which the concept of implication is wider than that of logical implication. Further, if we compare logical implication with implication, we find that if a proposition logically implies another then it also implies that other, but its converse is not true. A proposition may be implied by but not logically implied by another. This is the sense in which the concept of implication is wider than that of logical implication.

If it is true that a "logical implication" or "entailment" stands for a necessary connection between propositions then "implication" stands for some connection or other and "material implication" stands for no connection whatsoever. If it had been the case that the causal proposition expressed no connection whatsoever, then it could be translated as a material implication. If it had been the case that the causal proposition expressed a strict necessary connection, it could be translated as a logical implication. Since both these attempts are unsatisfactory, causal proposition must not be so translated. The statement "p causally implies q" indicates that p is causally necessary and sufficient for the truth of q. To say that p is causally necessary and sufficient for the truth of q is also to say that p is physically necessary and sufficient for the truth of q, and consequently, it cannot be identified with the implication that takes into considerations, only *logical* conditions. Logical implication or entailment holds between propositions that are strictly connected. Again, we cannot identify causal implication with material implication, for the truth of a material implication is not affected in the absence of the relevance of the two component parts of an implication. In the absence of any relevance between its parts, a material implication remains true; it cannot account for a causal connection. So we can find a similarity between the relation of causal implication and implication. Like implication, causal implication is stronger than the material implication but weaker than the logical implication. Consequently, causal implication is a material implication plus something, i.e. it is a material implication with a difference.

Our logical difficulties are not yet over. Can causal propositions be expressed in logical terms? It is a fundamental problem and its solution has not yet been found. Following the above line of thinking, it may possibly be claimed that since extensional logic is not concerned with the content of the propositions, it cannot adequately express causal propositions. It is true that philosophers' arguments about causes and causal relations are intelligible on the assumption that causes and causal relations are concerned with events. For example, Davidson is of opinion that the question of expressing causal relation by the extensional material condition is misleading. It confuses two separate matters: the logical form of causal statements and the analysis of causality. But this is a different point and we are not going to discuss it further. Finally, causal relation—if it is expressible in logical terms—its expression must be in between extensional and logical language; no amount of formalization should be expected to *solve* the problem of expressing causal relation in a logically satisfactory way.

5. Causal and Non-Causal Enquiries

Causal explanation is an explanation of events. Since events may either be natural or non-natural (among which are included human actions), so a real causal enquiry is fit for the explanation of the happening of natural events. This explanation is not possible, if and only if, if we take the help of mere formal logical instruments. As the process of explanation is different in different domains which we have shown elsewhere, the question that normally arises may be put in this way: is there any dichotomy between the enquiries of causal and non-causal domains? This is so because causal analysis is, to some extent, factual analysis, whereas non-causal analysis is more or less ethical, contextual, etc. Regarding the relation of the explanation of natural events and non-natural actions, two opinions are possible.

(1) There is the unity of the analysis of the natural events and non-natural actions.

(2) There is the discontinuity of the analysis of physical events and human actions.

The phrases "unity" and "discontinuity" of the analysis of physical events and human actions are used with reference to the nature of the *intelligibility* of the factual and normative aspects of the world. The theory of the unity of the enquiries of natural events and non-natural actions is supported by the argument that the rationality of both these types of events consists in a similar process.

Hempel, for instance, holds[85] the view that there are two basic types of scientific explanation of natural events, viz., deductive nomological explanation and probabilistic explanation. Deductive-nomological explanation states that the events to be explained are to be expected by reason of certain explanatory facts. An explanation of a particular event is often conceived as specifying its cause or causes. The causal explanation implicitly claims that there are general laws by virtue of which the occurrence of the causal antecedents is a sufficient condition for the occurrence of the event to be explained. So, causal enquiry is a deductive-nomological enquiry. The second type of scientific explanation is called probabilistic explanation. This kind of explanation is nomological because it accounts for a given phenomenon by reference to general laws and all of these are of probabilistic statistical form. But, as these laws are statistical rather than strictly universal, the resulting explanatory argument is inductive rather than deductive in character. We agree with Hempel in stating that causal explanation is a kind of nomological explanation. It is time to ask what light the preceding enquiries can shed on the explanatory procedure used in the domain of human actions. Following Hempel, it can be said that explanation of human actions are nomological in import, at least, if not in explicit formulation. There are thinkers who refer to the explanation of an action in its underlying *rationale*. This kind of explanation achieved by specifying the rationale underlying a given action is widely held to be fundamentally different from nomological explanation which explains the natural events. Dray, for instance, opines that the task of a rational explanation is not to subsume the explanandum under general laws, but "to show that what has done was the thing to have done for the reasons given, rather than merely the thing that is done on such occasions in accordance with certain laws"[86]. Dray thinks that the underlying "principle of action" is a judgment of the form "when in a situation of type $c_1, c_2 \ldots c_n$ the thing to do is x". Hempel's interest is to modify the position of Dray by means of the complete analysis of the kind of "situation" referred to here. These situations must be taken to include at least three factors: (1) the purpose of the agent; (2) empirical circumstances in which the agent had to act; and (3) the principles of conduct to which the agent was committed. These three factors lead us to say that a rational explanation answers a question of the form "why did agent A do x?" by offering an explanation of the type as follows: A was in a situation C and, in situation C, the appropriate thing for him to do was x. But this does not provide good reasons for believing that A did in fact do X. To explain why A did, in fact do x, we have to refer to the underlying rationale not by means of a normative principle of action, but by the descriptive statements to the effect that at the time in question A was a rational agent, and that a rational agent, when in circumstances of the kind c, will always do x. The explanatory form becomes:

(1) A was in a situation of type C,
(2) A was disposed to act rationally,
(3) Any person who is disposed to act rationally,

when in a situation of type C, invariably does x.

What is more important to Hempel's account is that the above explanatory account conforms to the manner of a deductive or of a probabilistic nomological explanation. Explanation of human actions, therefore, essentially conforms to one or the other of the two basic types of the explanation of natural events. The suggestion involved in this analysis may be put in this form: the nature of understanding is basically the same in all areas of scientific enquiry, i.e. deductive and the probabilistic sketch of nomological explanation.

Hempel's inclusion of natural events and non-natural actions within a single unified schema is seriously objected to by Dray on several grounds. First, there is no reason to believe that all human actions are rational in the sense which Hempel has explored. There is no criterion of rationality which uniquely singles out one course of action as "the thing to do". To this, we may add that because of essential and intrinsic intentionality, human actions cannot be explained nomologically. This suggests a degree of discontinuity between the analysis of factual and ideal discourse. Let us take history as an instance of an ideal discourse. History is primarily concerned with human beings with what they have thought, believed and done. What is ordinarily known as historical events are in most cases found to be complexes of human actions, intentions and ideas.

Michael Oakeshott thinks[87] that their discontinuity lies precisely in the fact that while natural events with which factual discourse is concerned stand in need of causal explanation, non-natural human actions with which ideal discourse is concerned cannot be explained causally. The categories of cause and effect have frequently been used in history by various pro-naturalist thinkers, but the ordinary selection of general causes is not the instrument of explanation of historical events. There are thinkers who believe that the peculiarities of historical events demand a sort of explanation which goes beyond the category of cause and effect. The historical world, according to Oakeshott, knows no accident. Whatever happens in history has its necessary and sufficient reason. The only principle of explanation consonant with the other postulates of historical experience is, according to Oakeshott, the unity or continuity of history. It is the unity of history that must be regarded as a presupposition of historical thought. This means that every event is related and that every event is but a moment in a world. The idea of causal explanation of historical events follows from the presupposition that a single historical event may be abstracted from the world of history, and this presupposition is pointless. This is the reason for the denial of causal explanation in the realm of human actions. Oakeshott's presentation of human action welcomes a narrative explanation of historical events. The very idea of a full narration of an action is misleading. Every narration presupposes a point of view, selection, etc. We always make a distinction between "given" and "intelligible", "narration" and "explanation". Rationality is not given but achieved; it involves systematization, deduction and organisation. So, history is always historical judgment; and what is given and what is not given are both its constituents.

The possibility of a new sort of causal explanation of human action has been suggested by Dray[88], who states that an event may be causally explained without subsuming it under any law. To give and defend a causal explanation in history is not to bring what is explained under a law and it almost always involves a *descriptive account* of the actual course of events. But Dray was not aware of the difficulty consisting in ascertaining the *actual* course of events.

In considering the question of discontinuity of the analysis of natural events and non-natural actions, we come to the conclusion that it is true that there is a distinction between the causal explanation of natural events and the non-causal explanation of human actions or historical events but the distinction does not really possess the characters which other philosophers think. The distinction is one of degree and not of kind.

6. Unity between Causal and Non-Causal Explanations

Let us now pass to the positive account of the relation between explanation of human actions and the explanation of natural events and try to find out whether there is unity between the two or not.

In the first chapter, we have tried to establish the view that natural events can be explained hypothetico—deductively and an explanation is causal, if and only if, the hypothesis from which we deductively draw the conclusion is a causal hypothesis. Causal explanations always possess a hypothetico—deductive pattern. If by the term "cause" we mean that which is necessary and sufficient for the occurrence of a thing and if by explanation we mean (at least partially) an appeal to general principles, then an explanation of natural events must in most cases be *causal*. At the same time, perhaps, nobody would deny that under similar circumstances people sometimes do not behave similarly. To explain this it is not enough to correlate action with intentions, ideas, etc. The attending circumstances are also to be stated and it is the latter which make the relation between events and ideas, intentions, intelligible. Without any reference to context, ideas by themselves do not have sufficient explanatory power. Our contention may be put in this way: we should not think that "if (cause) → decision then (effect) → action follows"; rather, we should think "if D in the situation S, A follows". In fact, the concept of causality, because of its limitation, has a very limited role to play in the explanation of human actions. Historical "causes" are according to Popper, situations indicated (not fully stated) by the specific initial conditions. On this ground, it can be said that historical causes do not fulfil the condition of sufficiency; yet we may not accept the emphatic counsel to the effect that "cause" must be banished from history. The acceptance of the contextual pattern of explanation of human action is supposed to be a flexible variation of the hypothetico-deductive model. Its underlying logical structure is, in some cases, the same as that of the explanation of natural events. The explicandum is followed from a set of law-like statements in the nature of hypothesis and the set of existential statements. The fundamental difference between the two types of hypothesis is that in the field of natural events, the laws have to be stated explicitly, whereas in the field of human actions the laws are not stated explicitly; their truth is generally assumed. Given the appropriate "laws" and some simple initial conditions the happenings of natural events can be safely predicted but, given the logic of situation, the behaviour of social individuals cannot be safely predicted. The flexibility of situational logic is introduced by the detailed description of circumstances attending the event to be explained. One may say that the situational logic is an attempt to show that human intentions do follow logically from social presuppositions. But this is not correct. Human intentions do not follow from social presuppositions with that sort of necessity which characterises the relation of "heat" with "expansion". But from the structural identity of the two schema of explanation, it does not follow that if one of them comes under the category of "cause-effect", so does the other. And to argue thus is to argue the dichotomy of the explanation in terms of its "cause" and the explanation in terms of its "situations". But, is there anyway of resolving this dichotomy?

We do not possess the slightest desire to ignore the well-known distinction between natural events and non-natural human actions. But this distinction should not be confused with division. We also believe in the difference between the two types of explanation—hypothetico-deductive and contextual. At the same time, we believe neither in the complete unity nor in the complete discontinuity of the two types of explanation. Events and actions do not call for entirely different types of explanation. It may be contended that there is a *logical unity* between the two. These explanations differ so far as their subject matters are concerned but both of agree in their purpose. The task of those explanations is to make intelligible the world of events—sometimes natural and sometimes non-natural. In order to make the occurrence of natural events, intelligible the positive sciences explain them in terms of its *cause*, and in order to make the occurrence of human actions intelligible, the social sciences explain them in terms of *situations*. We also know that sometimes human actions are very complex and complicated and yet we try to make them rational. Sometimes we decide immediately. Yet we can make it *rational* by constructing a situational logic of our personality. Therefore, the actions that we think *irrational* can be made rational by the introduction of the inner characters of the person who acts, i.e. all these can be explained under a concept. *Rationality* or *intelligibility* is the claim of both types of explanation and this rationality constitutes the logical unity of events (natural) and actions (human). Whether or not they fulfil their claim is, however, a different question.

If *rationality* be the demand of these explanations then we can resolve the dichotomy of events and actions by presuming that the *rationality* of natural events and the *rationality* of human actions are the two sides of one and the same *"rationality"*. By the same logic, we can also argue that the explanation of natural events is logically continuous with the explanation of human actions. Finally, one thing that should be pointed out *at once* is this. The logical unity cannot be understood demonstratively, for we cannot prove by any logical means that one is logically continuous with the other. We can only *understand* them to be so. Otherwise we would not be able to make room for values, ideas, norms in the domain of facts, events and causes.

CHAPTER VII

A Review of the Received View of Causal Explanation in Actions and Events

I have not departed from my old views but my studies and reflections in the last twenty years have persuaded me to be more aware about the distinction between explaining natural events and non-natural human actions. I find with increasing interest and convictions that the distinction between the two realms deserves more sustained analysis than I could, or even possibly can now, give it. I am inclined to believe a sort of autonomy or quasi-autonomy of the human discourse, defending the basic character of the freedom of will in human action. Much of what I have said is not my present view. My main interest in this discussion is to clarify some of my previous ideas and this clarification, I think, will improve my future presentation.

In the concluding portion of my analysis, I have attempted to show that the dichotomy of the explanation of natural events and human actions can be resolved by presuming the concept of *rationality*. Since rationality is the claim of both these types of explanations, it constitutes the logical unity of natural events and non-natural human actions. But the question that naturally arises is: is there a single. uniform standard of rationality for all areas of enquiry? Perhaps not, for *rationality*, as such, is not meaningful. Different meanings of the concept of *rationality* are possible. Swinburne[89], for example, is of opinion that the concept of rationality is ambiguous; it has different kinds. Feyeraband[90] regards that there is no comprehensive rationality. Rationality, according to Popper. is the ability to criticize. Some thinkers are of opinion that rationality is verifiability. Thus a definite definition of the concept of rationality is difficult. if not impossible, because its contextual meaning is equally important. Rationality, from another viewpoint, may be absolute or relative. Absolutists thinkers like Plato and Hegel are in favour of the view of absolute rationality. This rationality is criteria-independent because in this sense, reason requires no other criterion for justification. That is why, this must not be human rationality. Whereas relative rationality is not criteria-independent, it is meaningful only with reference to some context or situation. On this assumption, no action, no decision can be declared as rational in all situations. In this connection, we would like to mention the view of Kant who holds that *reason* has two functions—the *theoretical* and the *practical*. Reason determines not only our thoughts or beliefs but also our actions. If theoretical reason determines what to believe, practical reason determines what to do. According to Kant, the main function of reason is that of giving a systematic coherent understanding of experience and of the world. This discussion proves that a single standard of rationality is not possible. It is relative in character. It is true that the primary locus of rationality is individual human being. Perhaps with less plausibility, rationality may be attributed to natural events. Theories of rationality are, after all, extracted from human experience. To have the concept of rationality is to possess the ability to distinguish between reasons and non-reasons in one's own and in others' cases. The notion of rationality is not agent-neutral. Reference to the agent is essentially involved in the concept of reason for performing an action. It is equally true that everything is not a reason for everything else. It must be a relevant reason and relevancy is not situation-invariant. It is a fact that the agent's reasons explain or make intelligible his action. This intelligibility is possible by knowing the reasons of his doing. It implies that an action can be rationalized from the agent's points of view. But it should be borne in mind that the relation between the agent's reason and its rationality is not a logical relation. Every reason for an action need not be necessarily related to the intended result of an action. It is not unreasonable to think that two rational persons may differ about the notion of rationality. Thus, rationality is intimately connected with reason and the concept of agency is essentially linked up with the concept of reason. What is more important is that that the concept of agency is less important in the explanation of natural events. In effect, the concept of rationality is not sufficient for resolving the dichotomy of the explanation of natural events and non-natural human actions.

With a view to establishing the above-mentioned claim, I would like to discuss the view of Donald Davidson who observes the relation between actions (mental events) and events (physical) from a different point of view. Actions, decisions, perceptions, memories are mental events. Davidson holds that mental events as a class cannot be explained by science. Teleological explanation of action differs from explanation in the natural sciences in the sense that laws are not necessarily involved in the explanation of action. Davidson's philosophy of anomalous monism follows from the fact that there are no strict laws to relate the mental with the physical event. Davidson puts it like this: "there are no strict deterministic laws of which mental events can be predicted".[91] This further suggests that the mental events are type-different from the physical events, so they do not come under the strict causal laws of the physical world. The deterministic laws of the world do not affect the mental world. But, the claim of Davidson is not same in different sections of his book (Mental Events), (1970) and PAM (Principle of Anomalous Monism). The claim that there are no psychophysical laws does not entail that mental events cannot be explained or predicted at all, since such events might be explained or predicted on the basis of pure psychological laws and these laws might themselves be strict and deterministic. There are several grounds for dissatisfactions with anomalous monism. Anomalous monism cannot show the scientific essences or natures of mental states, events and processes. Davidson also thinks that the agent's desires, beliefs and also his actions have purely physical descriptions, and they are at bottom identical with physical events. Mental events as causes of physical events must obey strict deterministic laws and hence must themselves physical events since only physical events obey strict deterministic laws— this analysis is questionable. Since this explanation of human actions transforms human actions into physical phenomena, it ceases to be an account of human actions. Actions may be generally understood as something people do-cause to happen, or otherwise bring about as distinguished from example what happens to them. This is why the idea of agency is central to the theory of action. This aspect of the analysis has been neglected by Donald Davidson. He explicitly states "monistic is my view. since it holds that mental events are physical events"[92]. At another place, he states that such ontological reduction does not imply mental properties are physical properties. In philosophy, it is misleading to characterize physical and mental as logically equivalent attributes that may be ascribed to the same phenomenon. Davidson had strong inclination for identify actions with a set of bodily movements. At the same time, Davidson allows the possibility that there are mental events which do not cause physical events. Davidson's anomalous monism denies that a person has two different categories of event properties—one of which is spiritual or immaterial—but refuses to say anything about the nature of mental activities. His entire account in the last analysis becomes an analysis of mere physical phenomena. He does not give any *ontological* status to mental events as distinguished from physical events. Davidson's inclination for identifying actions with bodily movements seems itself to be questionable. Actions are qualified by intentional states (mental). Therefore they cannot be treated in an extensional way like physical events. Davidson's view is that causal relations are essentially nomological and based on induction while our knowledge of reasons and actions is not usually dependent on induction or knowledge of serious laws. He accepts that laws are not necessarily involved in the explanation of human action but he believes that both sorts of explanation can invoke causal connections. But, in action, every person has his own ways of reasoning. The basic concept in these is reason. That is one of the reasons why the concept of *causation* as ordinarily understood in natural sciences has an unimportant role to play in decision making. Human actions can be understood only by finding out the reasons behind the thoughts and actions. We should not suppose that here we are seeking a causal explanation of whatever happening there are in which the agent is involved. The agent cannot be taken to be a subject to the laws of nature. Davidson would not succeed in establishing total determinism in the field of human actions. He says that the explanation of action in terms of the agent's reason for doing it is a "rationalization"[93]. But to offer a rationalization is not to offer a real justification. It is only an anaemic sense that the rationalization of action justifies it, since it only shows the same "from the agent's point of view". Thus, Davidson's analysis cannot provide a satisfactory account for determining the relation between mental and physical events. If mental events do not possess any separate ontological status, then the attempt to resolve the dichotomy of the explanation of natural events and non-natural actions is pointless.

My present thinking is in favour of the view that we cannot equate explanation of human actions with that of natural events. Causal explanations and reason explanations are different in respect of their form and function. The attempt to identify these two types of explanations is groundless. If we equate human actions with natural events, we could definitely misunderstand these concepts. A cause is that which is necessary and sufficient for the occurrence of a thing and in the case of reason—action explanation, we search for the reasons of the agent for the doing of that action. Causal explanation in its explanatory design does not accommodate the actions of individuals. We know explanations are answers to the question "why", and causal explanation de-emphasizes questions about "who", "why", "when" and "where". These questions are very relevant to the study of the actions of humans. Principles of human actions are not as strict as the propositions of natural science. Laws of science are more rigorous than human or social laws. Human decisions play an important role in human reasoning, whereas in the case of scientific reasoning, decision plays an unimportant part. The actecedents and consequences of both these types of explanation are related differently. There may indeed be many differences of detail between the hypothesis of rationality and the many working hypotheses we use in other than the natural sciences. The differences between these principles may be only in degree but it is so important that it must not be lost sight of. Human actions are not mere happenings or events— they have meanings also. The meaning is that the manner in which a particular action performed and perceived by the agent. It is not true that everything that an agent does is rational. There must be something which is normal for the agent, and the normal for the agent is rational for him. Thus, in the case of the explanation of human action, there is no escape from the assumption of rationality. This rationality accepts relativism of all sorts and resists any imposition of universality. Man is not an eternally fixed property like a thing. His actions cannot be understood in terms of physiology or Biology alone. He acts neither like a machine nor like a mind alone. Consequently. we have to consider the different modes of enquiry for understanding human actions.

Now, when we are concerned with the relation between the explanation of natural events and non-natural human actions in the specific context of our time, it would be profitable to explain the concept of human action. The word "action", is ambiguous. By "action" we mean embodied mental action. Philosophers have used the word in different senses. Actions are what we do; actions must not be confused with practice. Practice may not be necessarily practical, it may also be theoretical. The peculiarity of action seems to consist in its autonomy as relatively free in character or origin. Actions need not have any past story behind them. The notion of action—as it is used in physics—is different from what we mean by human action. Actions are external changes. But. without effecting a change in the external world I act, I do something. Human action expresses a notion so fundamental that it is extremely difficult to explicate it in exact terms. One cannot clearly show action. Actions do not come into being suddenly. In the case of action, there is an inseparable experience of my doing it. This doing can be an object of moral evaluation. Nothing could be an instance of human action if no human being did it. Two human actions may be different even if the bodily movements are same. In the human context, it is difficult to conceive an action without a body. Actions exhibit some feature like end-consciousness which are more or less absent in different forms of animal action. That is why, action is body-linked. Those who defend the concept of mental act as distinguished from that of physical act do not contradict the view that mental acts such as thinking, believing need a physical body. Perhaps it is more than a body. It has some ability in it which enables it to be an agent. Any and everybody cannot act. Even living body as such is not sufficient for performing an action. Reference to intention is also necessary in determining the boundary of human action. In every action, it makes sense not only to ask "who did it" but also "why did he do it"? The logic of action demands the answer to the two questions about them. The purpose of these questions is to claim the reasons for actions alone. Mere awareness of bodily identity cannot enable men or animal to initiate and execute what may be called human action. Ordinarily, human body is distinguished from the mind, self or soul. It is difficult to deny the existence of physical states and mental states and their distinction. It is also true that behaviourists identify physical states with mental states. But there are some hard cases for which this identification cannot be justified. Sub-human animals have some rudimentary form of freedom but they cannot form what we human call cultural group. Generally speaking, freedom is ascribed to a person, self or soul. Spontaneity is indicative of an active ability of mind. It is primarily the ability of self-transcendence that lies at the roof of human action. Though transcendence is there in every sense of freedom, it must not be confused with the sense of Kant. In this sense, only adult rational human beings are free and responsible. We are free enough from the influence of our body to make ourselves responsible for our action including their mental component. A disembodied self cannot be regarded as a responsible agent or actor. That is why, the responsibility of the agent cannot be denied. In this aspect, we agree with the view of existentialists who hold that action is, by definition, transition from what I am to what I intend to be. The essence of a meaningful action is the presence of a "project."[94] Project is indeed an insight, an internal plan of human action. Man is not an eternally fixed property like a thing, and freedom of action is in the very nature of human being. According to Sartre[95]. liberty of the agent is the foundation and indispensable condition of all actions. Action, as opposed to mere happening, entails a motive. Nothing will count as action which is not so motivated. Sartre recognizes that the fundamental condition of all actions is the freedom of the agent. It is the exercise of freedom and the ability to shape the future that distinguishes man from all other beings that we know on earth. "Self as agent" is the central theme for existentialists. Freedom, decision and responsibility are prominent in the thinking of all existentialist thinkers. That is why they repudiate the mechanical or causal explanation of human actions. This discussion suggests that the causal world, which environs us, is entirely external to us. Any reductive approach of agency and action to physical phenomena destroys the very identity of human action as such. Consequently, as man's action is radically different from natural or physical phenomena, so his intelligibility must not be of the common pattern.

Actions have a different ontological status. Causality is not operative in the case of human actions. Responsibility or accountability is related to the concept of action. The notion of agency is here fundamental. In the case of explanation in the natural sciences, general truths are used as well as mentioned, whereas in the case of explanation in social sciences, general truths are not mentioned but only used. This is the basic difference between the explanations in two sciences. Hence, methodological unity is not possible, unification of knowledge cannot be accepted. Reduction to nature or to the mind, self or consciousness has elegance but, it also has advantages and disadvantages. Our experience is shaded and graded. Structural similarity between the intelligibility of human actions and natural events does not prove the unity between the two. Unification of knowledge is not defensible. In effect, a single pattern of explanation is not possible for all areas of enquiry.

CHAPTER VIII

A View of Indian Approaches

In this connection, it is instructive to discuss the Indian theory of *Karma* and *Karmaphala* (result of action) because it is an attempt to make intelligible action in moral terms. Belief in the law of *karma* has a great influence in the Indian philosophical thought. It is a law pertaining to action. It signifies that nothing can happen without a sufficient cause in the moral world. My objective in this analysis is to present a rough outline of the Indian concept of *Karma* (action) and its explanation. I shall not enter into any detailed analysis of the theory of *Karma* in Indian philosophical systems. With regard to its general form, I shall depend upon the discussions by some of the contemporary writers on Indian philosophy. Professors S. Radhakrishnan, S.N. Dasgupta, K.C. Bhattacharyya, M.Hiriyanna, S.C. Chatterjee, D.M. Datta, K.H. Potter, Daya Krishna, Rajendra Prasad are a few examples. The idea of *karma* constitutes one of the most distinctive features of Indian philosophical thinking. *Karma* literally means "what is done", "a deed". A characteristic of all voluntary deeds is that they are preceded by a desire for something which is described as their motive or phala.

Most systems of Indian philosophy accept in some form or the other their views regarding "*kārmic* causality", i.e. how actions lead to their consequences. By *kārmic* causality, it is meant that causal relation that is supposed to hold between actions (*karmas*) and their consequences or results (*karmaphala*) as reward and punishment for the agent. According to Rajendra Prasad[96], *karma* is here meant to be an intentional action, an action done with the intention to achieve something. All actions have consequences and whenever we perform an action, we perform it with the expectation of its possible consequences. This fact makes the action intentional. *Kārmic* causality manifests the truth that every person must bear the consequences of his actions and the quality of a person's life is determined by his past deeds. To think this is to realize that this law must be understood with reference to human actions.

Almost all Indian systems agree in accepting that whatever action is done by individual leaves behind some sort of potency and this has the power to arrange for him joy or sorrow in the future according to whether it is good or bad. In the Upaniṣad, it is said that men will have good or bad births due to his good or bad actions. As Rajendra Prasad observes[97], "karma, meaning intentional action, causes bondage is one of the basic principles or postulates of Classical Indian philosophy". Karma is the product of attachment. Mokṣa or freedom is regarded as freedom from births and deaths. Only embodied consciousness can be said to have saṃskāra or inductive habit of in it leading to action. Action done through the spirit of non-attachment would not produce any real karma. Pure consciousness cannot be regarded as responsible agent or actor. It cannot have any habit of traces of past actions in it leading to action. In this context we may refer to he view of Professor K.C. Bhattacharyya[98], "the jīvanmukta is one who after repeated births, repeated terms of probation passed successfully at least kills off all ignorance, all evils, and reaches absolute knowledge". That the liberated soul acquires no new karma has been accepted by all the philosophical schools which accept the law of karma.

With regard to the theory of karma, different philosophers" observations are of the following:

For Radhakrishnan[99], "According to the principle of karma, there is nothing uncertain or capricious in the moral world, we reap what we sow". Dasgupta said[100], "whatever action is done by an individual leaves behind some sort of potency which has the power to ordain for him joy or sorrow in the future according as it is good or bad". Hiriyanna[101] is of opinion that "whatever we knowingly do, will sooner or later bring us the result we merit: and there is no way of escape from it, what we sow, we must reap".

In Indian philosophy, the yoga philosophers[102] classified four kinds of karma, white (śukla), black (kṛṣṇa), white—black (śukla-kṛṣṇa) and neither black nor white (a śukla-kṛṣṇa). It is a causal fact that Śukla karmas (good actions) lead to happiness and the actor enjoys the joys and sorrows as the results of his actions. The last kind of actions—for the yogas—is not associated with any desire for the result. The yogas also believe that all *karmas* come from five fold tendencies (*kleśas*) namely *avidyā, asmitā, rāga, dvesa, abhiniveśa*. We perform a *karma* due to the vicious tendencies (*kleśa*) of the *buddhi*. The *karma* of the present life is the cause of the particular kind of future birth, the period of life and the pleasurable or painful experiences of future life. The Jaina thinkers[103] regard that karmas are certain sorts of infra-atomic particles of matter. *Karma* is produced from the actions of body, speech and mind. The Jainas believe that *karma* functions in such a manner that every change which takes place leaves a mark and it serves as the foundation of future action. The mīmāṃsakas[104] are of opinion that *karma* is the cause of bondage, when the cause is removed the effect necessarily ceases to be and it automatically results in restoring the self to its original state. The word *karma* is used as motion by the *vaiśeṣikas*. According to *śaṁkara*[105], individuality is due to *karma* which is a product of *avidyā*. Action presupposes agency but consciousness as such cannot be an agent or actor of the empirical world. For *vedāntins*, *karmas* cannot be ascribed to the absolute consciousness. Now, whatever be the nature of *karma*, it can be divided into three sections from a particular point of view. This division of *karma* is in accordance with the degree of maturation attained by them. *Prārabdha karma* is that part of which were done in the previous life but whose residues have matured to produce their results—the part that is unmanifested, i.e. those which were done in the previous life but whose residues have not yet matured and, therefore, have not yet began producing their consequences—are called *sañcita* and those which are done in the present life called *sañciyamāna*. In this connection, it is extementry important to note that all Indian schools which accept the law of *karma* also accept that the consequences of (at least) *Prārabdha Karmas* are inevitable. Through the attainment of true knowledge, the consequences of *sañcita* and *sañciyamāna karma* can be avoided but the situation is not same in the case of *prārabdha karmas*. Thus, so far as the consequences of *prārabadha karmas* are concerned, it can be said that it is difficult to get rid of them. In Indian systems, the law of *karma* is the law that exhibits the truth that there is no loss of the effect of work done. All actions of past, present and future will produce their proper results in this or another life of the individuals who act. But the problem is: how can an action produce an effect after a lapse of time? The *mīmāṃsāka* conception of *apūrva*, the law generates the future enjoyment of fruits of rituals performed now and the *Nyāya-vaiśesika* theory of *adṛṣṭa* the unseen principle, which brings out objects and events in accordance with moral principles. The yoga theory of *karmāśaya* (the bed of *karma* for the *puruṣa* to lie in) produces the appropriate consequences for the doer. The result that automatically follows from the theory of *karma* is that it implies determinism. If a man's past actions determine his present situation, then a man can never be totally free. But the point which is fundamental here is that that this determination must not be confused with law-like causal determination. In this connection, professor Mohanty[106] observes, "the Indian thinkers had to take recourse to the idea of super-sensible traces (*saṃskāras*) to make sense of translife causality and this is not causal explanation in the sense of a covering law-model nor could it have been arrived at by an inductive generalization."

The fact that natural causality is not identical with *Kārmic* causality, supported by the fact that the causal connections between actions and their consequences are supposed to be relative to agents and their situations but there is no evidence to support that natural process have this kind of dependence. *Kārmic* causality would relate an agent, an action, the result. In most cases, the ethical merit of actions is relative to the agents and their consequences. But natural causality, as we apprehend it, is not so agent-relative. Our common experience cannot support the relation between certain kinds of actions and certain kinds of results are fixed unless we assume that same things produce happiness or unhappiness in the same manner in every cases. But this assumption is not reasonable. In this connection, we can remind ourselves of professor K.C. Bhattacharyya's view who holds "natural law is but the obverse face of moral law"[107]. Hence, natural causality and *kārmic* causality must not be made identical.

Moreover, *kārmic* causality is different from intentional causality. Moral life suffers from endeavours. This life is a mode of living which is guided by interests and intelligence of man in the right direction. Men are more or less free to decide their courses of actions, make up their minds in a given situation and to develop their attitudes differently under different conditions. The relation between the goal intended and action done is non-causal. This approach of apprehending human action is certainly bound to remind us of a determination that is non-causal in character. Intentional determination is—as we have already seen—not a determination of the causal pattern. But *kārmic* determination is, as we understand, a causal determination. In effect, *kārmic* causality can neither be explained in terms of natural law-like determination nor be explained in terms of reasons. Reasons, motives and intentions are not causally but intentionally necessary for the intelligibility of human actions. *Kārmic* determination is an altogether different approach to the study of human actions. In this context Professor Mohanty states[108], "there is no *kārmic* science, there is a *kārmic* metaphysical point of view. As a metaphysical theory, it is capable of neither empirical confirmation nor empirical disconfirmation."

Moreover, the demand for moral intelligibility is, on this interpretation, subject to certain critical reflections. If moral intelligibility requires that each human being should reap only the fruits of his own actions, then no human being can really affect anyone else. Nobody can really be the cause of my joys and sorrows, nor can I be the cause of joys or sorrows of the others. This leads—according to Daya Krishna[109]—to "moral monadism". Moral monadism makes moral life impossible because morality gives emphasis on the care for others. It is true that our experience always goes against the monistic explanation of actions. Ordinarily, we accept the different causes of our sufferings and happiness. Some are due to our actions, some due to the actions of others and so on. But the theory of *karma* demands that if the world is to be morally intelligible, no one can reap the fruit of somebody else's actions. This is an important point no doubt, but, at the same time, it is not unreasonable to think that the transferribility or sharibility of the consequences of actions (karma) is somewhat limited, though not absolutely. Those who believe in the theory of karma might argue that one can and does suffer the consequences of other actions because he deserved it in virtue of some past actions he himself has done. This mode of reasoning may be questioned but we are not going to that debate. Thus, the above discussion indicates that transferribility or sharibility operates differently in the sphere of human actions and we can unhesitatingly conclude that whatever be the nature of *kārmic* determination it has a special significance for the intelligibility of human actions.

Notes and References

1. K.R. Popper, *The Logic of Scientific Discovery*, Hutchinson, London, Third Impression, 1962. PP. 59–62.
2. J.S. Mill, *The System of Logic*, Longmans, London, 1961, P. 305.
3. The Suggestive term, "Covering Law Model" borrowed from William Dray.
4. C.G.Hempel, "Deductive Nomological versus Statistical Explanation" in *Minnesota Studies in the Philosophy of Science*, H.Feigl and G. Maxwell (eds), Vol. 3, University of Minnesota Press, Minneapolis, 1962.
5. I. Scheffler, "Explanation, Prediction and Abstraction", "*The British Journal for the Philosophy of Science*, 1957, PP. 239–309; See also his *The Anatomy of Inquiry*, A. Knopf, New York, 1963.
6. M. Scriven, "Explanations, Predictions and Laws" in *Minnesota Studies in the Philosophy of Science*, H. Feigl and G. Maxwell (eds), Vol. 3, University of Minnesota Press, Minneapolis, 1962.
7. E. Nagel, *The Structure of Science*, Ch. XIV, Routledge and Kegan Paul, 1961.
8. R.B. Braithwaite, *Scientific Explanation*, Ch. IX, Cambridge University Press, 1968.
9. B. Russell, *Mysticism and Logic*, Ch. XI, George Allen and Unwin (c) Edition, 1963.
10. *Metaphysica* 1025^{b}27; see also *Physica*, 184^{a}10–14 translated into English under the editorship of W.D. Ross, Oxford at the Clarendon Press, Second Edition, 1928.
11. *Spinoza's Ethics*, Translated by Andrew Boyle, London: J.M. Dent and Sons, New York, E.P. Dutton and Co., 1959 (revised translation), Part-I and Part-II.
12. B. Russell, *Mysticism and Logic*, Ch. XI, See also his book *Human Knowledge, Its Scope and Limits*, Simon and Schuster, 1967, Ch. XI.
13. B. Russell, *The Problems of Philosophy*, New York, Oxford University Press, 1959, Ch. V.
14. C.D. Broad, *Man and its Place in Nature*, Routledge and Kegan Paul, 1951, PP. 452–457.

15. D. Hume, *An Enquiry Concerning Human Understanding*, Oxford University Press, L.A. Selby Bigge, Second Edition, 1962, See. 4.

16. *Immanuel Kant's Critique of Pure Reason*: Second Analogy, (Eng. Trans.) by N.K. Smith, Macmillan, 1964, PP. 218–233.

17. J.H. Woodger, *Biological Principles*, London, Routledge and Kegan Paul 1967, PP. 185–193, 441–448.

18. *Leibnitz, The Monadology and Other Philosophical writings*, (Eng.trans.) R. Latta, Oxford University Press, First edition, 1998, PP. 204–205, 235–238.

19. J.S. Mill, *A System of Logic*, BK.III, Ch. V.

20. *Immanuel Kant's Critique of Pure Reason*: The Second Analogy (Eng. Trans.) N.K. Smith, PP. 218–233.

21. K.R. Popper, *The Logic of Scientific Discovery*, Hutchinson, London, Third Impression, P. 61.

22. K.R. Popper, "Natural Laws and Contray-to-fact Conditionals", *Mind*, 1949, Vol. 58.

23. G. Ryle, *The Concept of Mind*, Hutchinson, London, 1949, P. 117.

24. J.S. Mill, *A System of Logic*, Longmans, 1961, p. 201.

25. W. James, *Pragmatism*, Longmans, 1946, PP. 54–55.

26. C.G. Hempel, Aspects of Scientific Explanation and other Essays, in *The Philosophy of Science*, The Free Press, New York, 1965, PP. 264–270.

27. E. Nagel, *The Structure of Science*, Routledge and Kegal Paul, 1961. PP. 56–57.

28. Ibid., P. 49

29. M. Black, "Notes On Paradoxes of Confirmation", *Aspects of Inductive Logic*, J. Hintikka and P. Suppes (eds), North Holland Publishing Company, 1966.

30. W.C. Kneale, *Probability and Induction*, Oxford University Press, 1949, P. 72

31. A.N. Whitehead, *Science and the Modern World*, Cambridge University Press, 1926, Ch. III

32. R.B. Braithwaite, *Scientific Explanation*, Cambridge University Press, 1949, Ch. I.

33. K.R. Popper, "Philosophy of Science": A personal Report", *British Philosophy in the Mid Century*, C.A. Mace (ed.), London, George Allen and Unwin, 1957.

34. B. Russell, *Human Knowledge, Its Scope and Limits*, Simon and Schuster, 1967, P. 308.

35. R. Carnap, *The Logical Structure of the World*, translated by R.A. George, London, Routledge and Kegan Paul, 1967, P. 263.

36. H. Reichenbach, *The Rise of Scientific Philosophy*, University of California Press, 1951, Ch. X, P. 157.

37. *Modern Philosophy of Science*, (edited and translated by Maria Reichenbach), Routledge and Kegan Paul, 1959, P. 132.

38. E. Nagel, *The Structure of Science*, Routledge and Kegan Paul, 1961, P. 73.

39. M. Knox, *Action*, George Allen and Unwin, London, 1968, Ch. V.

40. *The Nicomachean Ethics*, Translated into English under the editorship of W.D. Ross, Oxford at the Clarendon Press, Second Edition, 1928, BK. VI.

41. *Spinoza's Ethics and De-Intellectus Emendatine*, translated into English by Andrew Boyle, London; J.M. Dent and Sons, New York, E.P. Dutton Co. Inc. 1959, Pt. I

42. *De Corpore* (Quoted by R.S. Peter in his Hobbes, Harmondsworth, English, 1956), E_2 and also 121–22.

43. *De Corpore* (Quoted by R.S. Peter in his Hobbes) P. 206.

44. R.G. Collingwood, *An Essay on Metaphysics*, Oxford, 1940, PP. 285–95.

45. *Immanuel Kant's Critique of Practical Reason*, translated with and introduction by Lewis White beck, Bobbs Merill, the Liberal Arts Press, Inc., 1956, Pt. I, Bk. I, Ch. I, and see also *Kant's Groundwork of the Metaphysic of Morals*, translated and analyzed by H.J. Paton in the *Moral Law*, Hutchinson and Co., London, 1948, Ch. I, II, III.

46. A.I. Melden, *Free Action*, Routledge and Kegan Paul, London, 1961, Ch. IV.

47. P.H. Nowell Smith, *Ethics*, Penguin Books, 1954, PP. 125–26.

48. G. Ryle, *The Concept of Mind*, Hutchinson, London, 1949, P. 109.

49. S. Hamsphire, *Thought and Action*, The Viking Press, New York, 1960, Ch. 2.

50. C.G. Hempel, "Explanation in Science and in History" in *Philosophical Analysis and History*, (ed.), W.H. Dray, Harper and Row, 1966.

51. D. Davidson, *Essays on Actions and Events*, Clarendon press, Oxford, 1980, PP. 274–75.

52. D. Davidson, *Essays on Actions and Events*, Clarendon press, Oxford, 1980, P. 205.

53. J. Locke, *An Essay Concerning Human Understanding*, Oxford at the Clarendon Press, abridged and edited by A.S. Pringle Pattison 1924, Bk II, Ch XXVI, Sec. I

54. M. Bunge, *Causality*, Harvard, 1959, PP. 22–24

55. A. Einstein, *The World as I See it*, translated by A. Harris, London, England, 1935, Pt. V, PP. 146–161.

56. A.J. Ayer, *The Foundations of Empirical Knowledge*, London, Macmillan, 1940, Ch.IV, PP. 207–220.

57. M. Schlick, "Causality in Everyday life and in the Recent Science", *Readings in Philosophical Analysis*, H. Feigl and W. Sellars (eds), New York, 1949.

58. M.J. Adler, *The Idea of Freedom*, Garden City New York, Doubleday and Co. Inc., 1958, Pt. II, BK. II, Ch. III.

59. H. Ofstad, *An Enquiry Into the Freedom of Decision*, London: George Allen and Unwin, 1961, P. 33.

60. D. Hume, *An Enquiry Concerning Human Understanding* (L.A. Selby-Bigge, Second Edition), Oxford University Press, 1962, Pt. I, Sec. VIII.

61. D. Hume, *An Enquiry Concerning Human Understanding*, foot note 1, P. 94.

62. J.S. Mill, *A System of Logic*, Longmans, New Impression, 1961, Bk VI, Ch.II.

63. A.J. Ayer, *Philosophical Essays*, London, Macmillan, 1954, Ch. XII.

64. M. Schlick, *The Problem of Ethics*, translated by D. Rymin, Dover Publications, 1962, Ch. VII

65. B. Russell, *Philosophical Essays*, London, George Allen and Unwin (c) 1966, Ch. I, Sec-4.

66. M. Black, "Making Something Happen", *Determinism and Freedom*, S. Hook (ed.), New York University Press, 1958.

67. *Spinoza's Ethics and De Intellectus Emendatione*, translated by Andrew Boyle, London, J.M. Dent and Sons., New York, E.P.Dutton, Revised translation, 1959, Part I, II.

68. R. Latta (trans.), *Leibnitz the Monadology and the Philosophical Writings*, Oxford University Press, 1958, PP. 235–244.

69. B. Blanshard, "The Case for Determinism", *Determinism and Freedom*, S. Hook (ed.), New York University Press, 1958.

70. G. Ryle, *The Concept of Mind*, Ch. III.

71. K. Marx, *A Contribution to the Critique of Political Economy*, translated by N.I. Stone, Chicago, 1904.

72. *Philosophy of History*, Dover edition, P. 13.

73. *Kant's Critique of Pure Reason* translated by N.K. Smith and see also *Kant's Critique of Practical Reason*, translated by L.W. Beck.

74. P.F. Strawson, *Individuals*, London, Methuen, 1959, Pt. I , Ch. III.

75. C.D. Broad, *Ethics and the History of Philosophy*, London, Routledge and Kegan Paul, 1952, Sec. 3, PP. 210–211.

76. M. Schlick, "Causality in Everyday life and in Recent Science" in *Readings in Philosophical Analysis*, H. Feigl and W. Sellars (eds), New York, 1949.

77. A.J. Ayer, *The Problem of knowledge*, London, Macmillan and Penguin Books, 1956, Ch. IV.

78. A.J. Ayer, *The Problem of Knowledge*, London, Macmillan, 1956, P. 194.

79. M. Bunge, *Causality*, Harvard University Press, 1959, PP. 35–52.

80. J.S. Mill, *A System of Logic*, Longmans (New Impression), 1961, P. 217.

81. Bhasapariccheda, 17–18

82. F.P. Ramsey, *The Foundation of Mathematics*, New York, 1931, P. 197.

83. A.C. Ewing, *Non-linguistic Philosophy*, George Allen and Unwin, London, 1968.

84. G.P. Henderson, "Causal Implication" *in Mind*, 1959.

85. C.G. Hempel, "Explanation in Science and in History", *Philosophical Analysis and History*, W.H. Dray (ed.), Harper and Row, 1966.

86. W.H. Dray, *Laws and Explanation in History*, Oxford, 1957, Ch. V.
87. M. Oakeshott, "Historical Continuity and Causal Analysis" *Philosophical Analysis and History*, W.H. Dray (ed.), Harper and Row, 1966.
88. W.H. Dray, *Laws and Explanation in History*, Oxford, 1957, Ch. V.
89. R. Swinburne, *Faith and Known*, Oxford University Press, 1981, P. 33
90. Paul Feyeraband, *Science in a Free Society* (Vesco Edn.), London, 1983.
91. D. Davidson, *Essays on Actions and Events*, Clarendon Press, Oxford, 1980, P. 208.
92. Davidson's, "Reply to J.J.C. Smart" P. 245.
93. D. Davidson, *Essays on Actions and Events*, Clarendon Press, 1980, P. 3.
94. Maurice Natanson (ed.), *Phenomenology and the Social Sciences*, Vol. II, North Western University Press, Evaston, 1973, PP. 145–146.
95. *Six Existentialist Thinkers* by H.J. Blackham, (Routledge and Kegan Paul), London and Huxley, 1952, P. 127.
96. Rajendra Prasad, *Karma, Causation and Retributive Morality* Indian Council of Philosophical Research, New Delhi, 1989, P. 213
97. Ibid., P. 238
98. K.C.Bhattacharyya, *Studies in Philosophy*, Gopinath Bhattacharyya, (ed.), Motilal Banarsidass, Delhi, 1983.
99. S. Radhakrishnan, *Indian Philosophy* Vol. I, New York, Macmillan Company, London, George Allen and Unwin (Ltd) 1962, P. 245.
100. S.N. Dasgupta, *A History of Indian Philosophy*, Vol.I, Cambridge the University Press, 1951, P. 71.
101. M. Hiriyanna, *Essentials of Indian Philosophy*, Prentice Hall, Inc. 1963. P. 48.
102. S.N. Dasgupta, *A History of Indian Philosophy* Vol. I, Cambridge at the University Press, 1951, P. 73.
103. Ibid., P. 73, P. 192.
104. M. Hiriyanna, *Outlines of Indian Philosophy*, Blackie and Son Publishers (P) Ltd, Mumbai Delhi, Chennai, P. 334.
105. S. Radhakrishnan, *Indian Philosophy* Vol. II The Macmillan Company, London, George Allen and Unwin (Ltd), 1962, P. 634.
106. J.N. Mohanty, *Reason and Tradition in Indian thought*, An Essay on the Nature of Indian Philosophical Thinking, Clarendon press, Oxford, 1992, P. 266.
107. K.C. Bhattacharyya, *Studies in Philosophy*, Gopinath Bhattacharyya (ed.), Motilal Banarsidass, Delhi, 1983, P. 59.
108. J.N. Mohanty, *Reason and Tradition in Indian thought*, An essay on the nature of Indian Philosophical Thinking, Oxford, 1992, P. 266.
109. Daya Krishna, *Indian Philosophy*, A Counter Perspective, Delhi, Oxford University Press, Oxford, New York, 1991, P. 178.

Select Bibliography

Adler, M.J., *The Idea of Freedom*, Garden City New York, Doubleday and Co.,1958.

Ayer, A.J., *The Foundations of Empirical Knowledge*, London, Macmillan, 1940.

————, *Philosophical Essays*, London, Macmillan, 1954.

————, *The Problem of Knowledge*, London: Macmillan and Penguin Books, 1956.

Barlingay S.S., *Reunderstanding Indian Philosophy*, D.K. Print World (P) Ltd., New Delhi, 1998.

Beck, L.W. (tr.), *Immanuel Kant's Critique of Practical Reason*, Bobbs Merill, 1956.

Bhadra, M.K., *A critical study of Sartre's Ontology of Consciousness*, The University of Burdwan, 1978.

Bhattacharyya, K.C., *Studies in Philosophy*, (ed.) Gopinath Bhattacharyya, Motilal Banarsidass, Delhi, 1983.

Black, M.(ed.), *Philosophical Analysis*, Ithaca, 1950.

Blackham,H.J., *Six Existentialist Thinkers*, Routledge and Kegan Paul, London, Huxley 1952.

Boyle, A.(tr.), *Spinoza's Ethics and De Intellectus Emendatione*, London, J.M. Dent and Sons, 1959.

Bradley, F.H., *The Principles of Logic*, Oxford University Press, 1922.

Braithwaite, R.B., *Scientific Explanation*, Cambridge University Press, 1968.

Broad, C.D., *Ethics and the History of Philosophy*, London, Routledge and Kegan Paul, 1952.

————, *Mind and its Place in Nature*, Routledge and Kegan Paul, 1951.

Bunge, M., *Causality*, Harward University Press. Harvard, 1959.

Bunge, M.(ed.), *The Critical Approach to Science and Philosophy*, New York, 1964.

Campbell, A.C., *In Defence of Free Will*, London, George Allen and Unwin, 1967.

Carnap, R., "Testability and Meaning" in *Philosophy of Science*, Vol. III, 1936 and Vol. IV, 1937.

Chattopadhyaya,D.P., *Individuals and Societies*: A Methodological Enquiry, Allied Publishers, Mumbai, Kolkata, 1967.

————, *Individuals and Worlds*, Essay in Anthropological Rationalism, Delhi, Oxford University Press, London, New York, 1976.

_____, *Anthropology and Historiography of Science*, Ohio University Press, Athens, 1990.

_____, *Induction, Probability and Skepticism*, State University of New York Press, 1999.

_____, *Philosophy of Science Phenomenology and other Essays*, Indian Council of Philosophical Research, New Delhi, 2003.

Chisholm, R.M., "Contrary-to-Fact Conditionals" in *Reading in Philosophical Analysis*, H. Feigl and W. Sellars (eds), New York, 1949.

Cohen, M., *Reason and Nature*, New York, 1931.

Collingwood, R.G., *An Essay on Metaphysics*, Oxford, 1940.

Dasgupta, S.N., *A History of Indian Philosophy* Vol. I, II, Cambridge University Press, 1951.

Davidson, D., *Essays on Actions and Events*, Clarendon Press, Oxford, 1980.

Dray, W.H., *Laws and explanation in History*, Oxford, 1959.

_____ (ed.), *Philosophical Analysis and History*, Harper and Row, 1966.

Einstein, A., *The World as I see it*, A Harris (tr.) London, England, 1935.

Ewing, A.C., *Non-Linguistic Philosophy*, George Allen and Unwin, London, 1968.

Feigl, H. and Maxwell, G. (eds), *Minnestota Studies in the Philosophy of Science*, Vol. III (eds), University of Minnesota Press, 1962.

Feigl, H. and Sellars, W. (eds), *Readings in Philosophical Analysis*, 1949.

Feigl, H. and Broadbeck, M. (eds), *Readings in the Philosophy of Science*, New York, 1953.

Feyeraband, P.K., "Explanation, Predictions and Laws" in *Minnesota, Studies in the Philosophy of Science*, Feigl, Scriven and Maxwell (eds), Minnesota University Press, 1962.

Feyeraband, P., *Science in a Free Society*, (Vesco Edn), London, 1983.

Flew, A.G.N. (ed.), *Essays on Logic and Language*, Oxford; Blackwell, Second series, 1953.

_____, *Hume's Philosophy of Belief*, London, 1961.

Frank, P., *Philosophy of Science*, Prentice Hall, 1957.

_____, *Between Physics and Philosophy*, Cambridge, Harvard University Press, 1941.

George, R.A. (tr.), *The Logical Structure of the World* (R. Carnap.), London, Routledge and Kegan Paul, 1967.

Goodman, N., *Fact, Fiction and Forecast*, Harvard University Press, 1941.

Gupta, K.C., *A Critical Examination of Marxist Philosophy*, Kolkata, 1962.

Hampshire, S., *Thought and Action*, London, 1960.

_____, *Spinoza*, Pelican, 1965,

Hart, H.L.A. and Honoré, *Causation in the Law*, Clarendon Press, Oxford, 1959.

Harre, R. and Madden, E.I., *Causal Powers*, A theory of natural necessity, Basil, Blackwell, Oxford, 1975.

Hegel, G.W.F., *The Philosophy of History*, Dover, 1956.

Hempel, C.G., *Aspects of Scientific Explanation*, New York, 1965.

———, *Philosophy of Natural Science*, Prentice Hall, 1966.

Hintikka, J. and Suppes, P. (eds), *Aspects of Inductive Logic*, North Holland, Publishing Company, 1966.

Hiriyanna, M., *Essentials of Indian Philosophy*, Prentice Hall, Inc.,1963.

———, *Outlines of Indian Philosophy*, Blackie and Son Publishers (P) Ltd., Mumbai, Delhi, 1983.

Hook, S.(ed.), *Determinism and Freedom*, New York University Press, 1958.

———, *Towards the understanding of Karl Marx*, New York, 1933.

Hospers, J., *An Introduction to Philosophical Analysis*, Routledge and Kegan Paul, 1956.

Hume, D.,*An Enquiry Concerning Human Understanding* Oxford University Press, L.A. Selby Bigge, Second Edition, 1962.

———, *A Treatise of Human Nature*, Everyman's Library, London, 1911.

James, W., *Pragmatism*, Longmans, 1946.

Joseph, H.W.B., *An Introduction to Logic*, Prentice Hall, 1966.

Korner, S., *Kant*, Pelican, 1960.

Kneale, W.C., *Probability and Induction*, Oxford University Press, 1949.

Knox, M., *Action*, George Allen and Unwin, London, 1968.

Krishna, Daya., *Indian Philosophy,* A Counter Perspective, Delhi, Oxford University Press, Oxford, New York, 1991.

Lakatos, T. (ed.), *The Problem of Induction*, Amsterdam, 1968.

Latta, R. (tr.), *Leibnitz, the Monadology and other Philosophical Writings*, Oxford University Press, 1898.

Lewis, C.I., *Mind and the World Order*, New York, Seribner, 1929.

Lewis, C.I., and Langford, C.H., *Symbolic Logic*, New York, Dover, 1959.

Locke, J., *An Essay Concerning Human Understanding*, Oxford at the Clarendon Press, abridged and edited by A.S.Pringle-Pattison, 1924.

Lycan, W.G.,*Judgement and Justification*, Cambridge University Press, Cambridge, 1988.

Mackie, J.L., *Truth, Probability and Paradox, Studies* in Philosophical Logic, Oxford at the Clarendon Press, 1973.

Mahajan, G., *Explanation and Understanding in the Human Sciences*, Oxford University Press, Oxford, 1992.

Matilal, B.K., *Perception*, An Essay on Classical Theories of Knolwedge, Clarendon Press, Oxford, 1986.

Melden, A.I., *Free Action*, Routledge and Kegan Paul, London, 1961.

Mill, J.S., *A System of Logic*, Longmans, 1961.

Mohanty, J.N. *Reason and Tradition in Indian Thought*, Clarendon Press, Oxford, 1992.

Mure, G.R.G., *The Philosophy of Hegel*, Oxford University Press, 1965.

Nagel, E., *The Structure of Science*, Routledge and Kegan Paul, 1961.

Natanson, M. (ed.), *Phenomenology and the Social Sciences*, Vol. II, Northwestern University Press, Evaston, 1973.

Nowell Smith, P.H., *Ethics*, Penguin Books, 1967.

Oakeshott, M., "Historical Continuity and Causal Analysis" in *Philosophical Analysis and History* W.H. Dray (ed.), Harper and Row, 1966.

Ofstad, H., *An Enquiry into the Freedom of Decision*, London, George Allen and Unwin, 1961.

Pap, A., *Elements of Analytic Philosophy*, New York, Macmillan, 1949.

Passmore, J., *A Hundred Years of Philosophy*, London, Duckworth, 1957.

Paton, H.J. (tr.) *Kant's Groundwork of the Metaphysic of Morals*, Hutchinson and Co., London, 1948.

————, *The Categorical Imperative*, Hutchinson, London, 1963.

Pears, D.F., *Bertrand Russell and the British tradition in Philosophy*, London, 1968.

Peter, R.S., *Hobbes*, Harmondsworth, England, 1956.

Popper, K.R., *The Logic of Scientific Discovery*, Hutchinson, London, 1962.

————, "Philosophy of Science: A personal Report," *British Philosphy in the Mid Century* C.A. Mace (ed.) London, George Allen and Unwin, 1957.

————, *The Open Society and its Enemies*, Princeton; Princeton University Press, 1950.

————, *Conjectures and Refutations*, New York, Basic Books, 1962.

————, *The Poverty of Historicism*, Routledge and Kegan Paul, 1957.

Prasad, Rajendra., *Karma, Causation and Retributive Morality*, Indian Council of Philosophical Research, 1989.

Ramsey, F.P., *The Foundation of Mathematics*, New York, 1931.

Reichenbach, H., *The Rise of Scientific Philosophy*, University of California Press, 1951.

————, *Experience and Prediction*, Chicago University Press, 1938.

———— (ed.), *Modern Philosophy of Science*, Routledge and Kegan Paul, 1959.

Ross, W.D.(tr.), *Aristotle's Metaphysica*, Oxford at the Clarendon Press, Second Edition, 1928.

————, *Aristotle's Physica*, Oxford at the Clarendon Press, Second Edition, 1928.

————, *The Nicomachean Ethica*, Oxford at the Clarendon Press, 1928.

Russell, B., *Mysticism and Logic*, George Allen and Unwin, 1963.

————, *The Problems of Philosophy*, New York, Oxford University Press, 1959.

————, *Scientific Outlook*, George Allen and Unwin, 1954.

————, *The Analysis of Mind*, London, George Allen and Unwin, 1921.

————, *Our knowledge of the External World*, George London, Allen and Unwin, 1926.

Ryle, G., *The Concept of Mind*, Hutchinson, London, 1949.

Sartre, Jean-Paul, *Being and Nothingness*, (translated by Hazel E.Barnes) Washington Square Press, Inc., New York, 1966.

Scheffler, I., *The Anatony of Enquiry*, A Knopf, New York, 1963.

Schlick, M., "Causality in Everyday Life and in Recent Science" *Readings in Philosophical Analysis*, H.Feigl and W.Sellars (eds), New York, 1949.

————, *The Problems of Ethics*, D. Rymin (tr.), Dover Publications, 1962.

Scriven, M., "Explanations, Predictions and Laws" in *Minnesota Studies in the Philosophy of Science*, H. Feigl and G. Maxell (eds), University of Minnesota Press, Vol. III, 1962.

Sen, P.K., "The Concept of Rationality" in *Reference and truth*, Indian Council of Philosophical Research in Association with Allied Publishers, New Delhi, 1991.

————, *Logic, Induction and Ontology*, Essays in Philosophical Analysis, Macmillan, 1980.

Shoemaker, S., *Identity, Cause and Mind*, Philosophical Essays, Cambridge University Press,1984.

Sircar, T.K., *Knowledge, Truth and Justification*, Jadavpur Studies in Philosophy, Allied Publishers in collaboration with Jadavpur University, Kolkata, 1992.

Smith, N.K. (tr.), *Immanuel Kant's Critique of Pure Reason*, Macmillan, 1964.

Strawson, P.F., *Individuals*, London, Methuen, 1959.

————, *Introduction to Logical Theory*, University Paperbacks, Methuen, London, 1963.

Swinburne, R., *Faith and Reason*, Oxford University Press, 1981.

Articles

Burks, A.W., "The Logic of Causal Propositions" in *Mind*, 1951.

Chattopadhyaya,D.P., "Can Induction be Justified?," *The Journal of the Indian Academy of Philosophy*, Vol. VI, 1967.

————, "Rationality Culture and Values". In *The Journal of the Indian Council of Philosophical Research*, Vol. VIII, No. I, 1990.

————, "Towards a Philosophical Theory of Action," in H.Banerjee and T. Bandopadhyaya (eds), *Actions, Explanation and Interpretation Bagchi*, K.P. Kolkata, 1990.

Chaturvedi, Vibha, "Causality of Karmic Justice", *Journal of the Indian Council of Philosophical Research*, Vol. XVIII, No. 3, 2001.

Dummett, M., "Can an Effect Precede its Cause",? *Proceeding of the Aristotelian Society*, Supplementary Volumes, 1944.

Ewing, A.C., "What is Action?" in *Proceedings of the Aristotelian Society*, Supplementary Volume, XVIII, 1938.

———, "A Defence of Causality" in *Proceedings of the Aristotelia Society*, 1932–1933.

Henderson, G.P., "Causal Implication" in *Mind*, 1959.

Kneale, W.C., "Natural Laws and Contrary to fact Conditionals", *Analysis*, Vol. X, 1950.

Nayek, G.C., "Reason, Rationality and Irrational" in the *Journal of Indian Council of Philosophical Research*, Vol. VI, No. I, 1988.

Popper, K.R., "Natural Laws and Contrary-to-fact conditionals, in *Mind*, Vol. LVIII, 1949.

Rescher, N., "Belief Contravening Suppostions" *in Philosophical Review*, 1961.

Sen, P.K., "Laws of Logic and Rules of Inference" in the *Journal of the Indian Academy of Philosophy*, Vol. VII, No. I, 1968.

———, "The Analytic view of Entailment", in the *Journal of the Indian Academy of Philosophy*, Vol. II, 1963.

———, "Entailment, Necessity and Formal Implication" in the *Journal of Indian Academy of Philosophy*, Vol. VI, 1967.

Sengupta, K., "Bad News for Causal Explanations of Human Behaviour" in the *Journal of the Indian Council of Philosophical Research*, Vol. VI, No. I, 1988.

Index